+ + +

EASY
VEGAN

+ + +

+ + +

EASY VEGAN

+ + +

140 vegan dishes,
from everyday to gourmet

SUE QUINN

Photography by Victoria Wall Harris

murdoch books

Sydney | London

contents

+ + +

introduction

+ + +

Why do growing numbers of people seem to be adopting a vegan diet? Some people are removing animal fat from their diet to reduce the risk of heart disease and for other health reasons, while others are approaching veganism from an animal welfare perspective. Eating less meat is also recognised as environmentally friendly because plant foods require less land and water to produce.

Whatever your motivations, moving to a plant-based diet requires a little planning, but it isn't the quantum leap into alien eating territory that many people think. Before I started writing this book, I feared that eating a vegan diet equated to deprivation. But once I began to explore plant-based recipes, I realised that it's not about missing out at all.

The truth is that a lot of our eating patterns are based on habits that are as easy to give up as they were to pick up in the first place. Giving up meat, fish and other animal products might feel like a wrench to start with, but if you fully explore plant-based eating you could end up enjoying a more varied diet than you ever did before.

how to be vegan

+ + +

WHAT IS A VEGAN DIET?

A vegan diet is made up entirely of plant-based ingredients and excludes products derived from animals. It is based on:

+ NO MEAT, FISH OR ANIMAL PRODUCTS, SUCH AS ANIMAL FAT OR GELATINE

+ NO DAIRY PRODUCTS, SUCH AS COW OR GOAT'S MILK, CHEESE OR YOGHURT

+ NO EGGS

+ NO HONEY

How to begin?

There's no best way to start a vegan diet. One option is to go straight in and eat an entirely plant-based diet from the start. Alternatively, ease into vegan eating by starting with one plant-based meal a day, or one plant-based eating day each week. Some people just like to eat vegan after 6 pm! Just choose the method that's right for you.

Whatever approach you take, life will be easier and tastier if you have the right ingredients on hand. Stock up on fresh fruit and vegetables, and choose your favourite items from the shopping list on pages 14–15. Remember that if you pack your meals with flavour you're less likely to pine for animal products, so don't stint on herbs and spices.

Chances are that some of your favourite dishes are already plant-based or can easily be veganised, so focus on including these when planning your meals.

Start swapping dairy milk for plant milk on cereal – you really won't notice the difference after a day or two. Or grate vegan cheese onto your vegetable pasta dish instead of parmesan cheese. You might be surprised at how little you have to adapt some of the meals you already enjoy.

Eating right

A vegan diet is not automatically a healthy one. Chips (crisps) and sweets can be vegan, but a diet based on junk food obviously isn't nutritious. However, a well-planned vegan diet can contain all the elements of healthy eating.

Make sure you consume high-fibre, low-kilojoule foods such as fruit, vegetables, grains and legumes balanced with some high (good) fat foods such as oils, nuts, avocados and dried fruit. Eat lots of brightly coloured fruit and vegetables; less colourful bananas and potatoes are useful sources of protein but lack important nutrients. Also make sure there are plenty of starchy foods (potatoes, rice, grains, bread) and beans and pulses in the mix.

Carefully read the nutrition chart on the opposite page and factor in this information when planning your diet. If you remove animal products from your cooking it is crucial that you know how to obtain all the nutrients you need without them. In particular, vegans need to ensure they eat enough calcium, iron and vitamin B12. Pregnant women and nursing mothers should take specialist advice. Please note that the nutritional information applies to adults and not children.

vegan nutrition chart

	RECOMMENDED DAILY INTAKE FOR ADULTS	SOURCES FOR VEGANS (Source: Vegan Society UK)
vitamin B12	Varies from country to country, from 1.5 micrograms (UK) to 2.4 micrograms (AU) and 3 micrograms (US) .	Dietary sources for vegans are limited. Cereals, nutritional yeast and soya drinks fortified with B12 are recommended.
calcium	700 micrograms*	Foods providing 100 mg calcium: 133 g spring greens 67 g curly kale (boiled) 42 g almonds 217 g boiled chickpeas 33 g tofu (made with calcium sulphate) 83 g fortified soya milk 40 g figs
vitamin D	5–15 micrograms** but varies from person to person.	Exposure to summer sunshine as well as fortified cereals, soya products and spreads. Winter supplements recommended.
iron	8.7 micrograms (men)* 14.8 micrograms (women)*	Foods providing 2 mg iron: 14 g pistachio nuts 32 g roasted cashew nuts 57 g lentils 95 g boiled chickpeas 19 g tahini 59 g dried apricots
omega-3	No official recommended daily allowance but a regular intake is acknowledged to help maintain a healthy heart.	Oils made from flaxseed (linseed), rapeseed and hemp seed.
iodine	140 micrograms	Seaweed is one of the best sources of iodine, but is highly variable in its content. Kelp is the best source.

* UK Department of Health's Reference Nutrient Intake for adult men and women
**Nutrient Reference Values for Australia and New Zealand

protein content of food

+ + +

The following table shows the approximate protein content of various plant-based foods. The recommended daily protein intake is 45 g for women and 55 g for men and each balanced meal should contain 1 protein element.

For approximate comparative purposes, the table below and on the opposite page shows the protein content of 1 serving of sirloin steak.

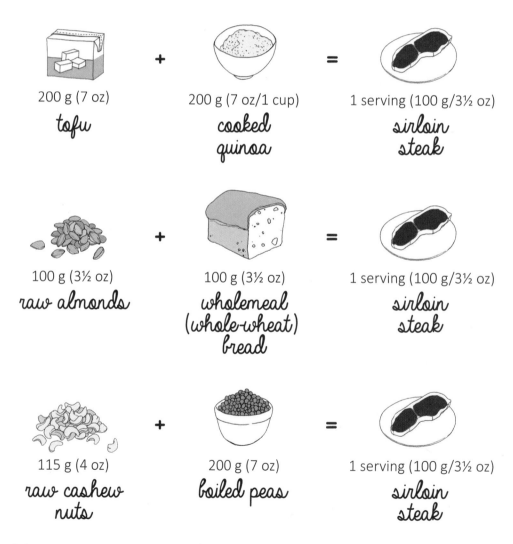

200 g (7 oz)
tofu

+

200 g (7 oz/1 cup)
cooked quinoa

=

1 serving (100 g/3½ oz)
sirloin steak

100 g (3½ oz)
raw almonds

+

100 g (3½ oz)
wholemeal (whole-wheat) bread

=

1 serving (100 g/3½ oz)
sirloin steak

115 g (4 oz)
raw cashew nuts

+

200 g (7 oz)
boiled peas

=

1 serving (100 g/3½ oz)
sirloin steak

INGREDIENT	AVERAGE GRAMS OF PROTEIN PER 100 G*		INGREDIENT	AVERAGE GRAMS OF PROTEIN PER 100 G*
sirloin steak	31 g		boiled peas	5 g
nutritional yeast	48 g		cooked quinoa	4 g
raw peanuts	26 g		kale	4 g
raw almonds	21 g		dried figs & apricots	3 g
raw cashew nuts	18 g		soya milk	3 g
tofu	11.5 g		brussels sprouts	3 g
wholemeal (whole-wheat) bread	10 g		broccoli	3 g
boiled chickpeas	9 g		asparagus	3 g
boiled lentils	9 g		cauliflower	2 g
dark chocolate (70%)	8 g		avocado	2 g

* Source: USDA National Nutrient Database; protein content for tofu has been averaged, as values vary widely according to type and brand; values for vegetables are for raw, unless stated otherwise

vegan celebrities

+ + +

CHRISTINE LAGARDE

Head of the IMF

TED DANSON

Actor

PRINCE

Singer

MICHELLE PFEIFFER

Actor

CARL LEWIS

Olympic track & field star

AVRIL LAVIGNE

Singer

SINEAD O'CONNOR

Singer

BEN STILLER

Actor

BILL CLINTON

Former US President

ANNE HATHAWAY

Actor

BRAD PITT

Actor

ALANIS MORISSETTE

Singer

shopping list

+ + +

A bountiful store cupboard makes preparing and enjoying vegan meals easier. You don't need to buy everything on this list – choose your favourites.

PLANT MILKS & YOGHURTS

VEGAN MARGARINE & MAYONNAISE

VEGAN CHEESE

TOFU & TEMPEH

WHOLE GRAINS like pearled barley, farro, spelt, buckwheat & quinoa

PASTA, RICE, NOODLES & COUSCOUS

DRIED MUSHROOMS

LENTILS

TINS OF BEANS, CHICKPEAS & TOMATOES

NUTS like cashew nuts, almonds & hazelnuts to make nut butters & milks

SEEDS like pumpkin, sesame, sunflower, flax & chia

DRIED FRUIT like cherries, cranberries, mulberries, apricots & raisins

RAPESEED, OLIVE, VEGETABLE & COCONUT OILS

SWEETENERS like agave nectar, molasses, brown rice syrup, dates, date syrup, maple syrup & sugar

HERBS, SPICES & CHILLIES

VEGAN SAUCES & CONDIMENTS such as chilli sauce, chipotle paste, harissa paste, mustard, yeast extract & soya/tamari sauce

VEGAN STOCK (BOUILLON) CUBES OR STOCK (BOUILLON) POWDER

CEREALS like rolled (porridge) oats & quinoa flakes

VEGAN CHOCOLATE & GOOD-QUALITY COCOA POWDER

VEGAN SPECIALTIES (see opposite)

nutritional yeast

egg replacement powder

mushrooms

coconut oil

nut milk

AGAR-AGAR – a flavourless thickening agent made from seaweed extracts. Available in powder, flakes and bars.

AGAVE NECTAR – a syrupy sweetener made from the agave plant.

COCONUT OIL – white and solid at room temperature, and available refined and unrefined. Refined is processed to remove the coconut smell and flavour, and has a higher smoke point, making it more suitable for frying. Some people prefer unrefined due to the chemicals sometimes used in the refining process.

DRIED MUSHROOMS – such as porcini, oyster and shiitake add a rich and 'meaty' flavour to cooking. Must be rehydrated in hot water before cooking.

FLAXSEEDS – also called linseeds, are an excellent source of omega–3 fatty acids. Use to make flax eggs (*see* p 17) instead of shop-bought egg replacer. Ground flaxseeds can quickly turn rancid, so keep refrigerated or only grind as and when needed.

almond milk

tempeh

flaxseeds

sugar

agar-agar powder

xanthan gum

soya milk

seitan

agave nectar

tofu

NUTRITIONAL YEAST – an edible deactivated yeast also known as 'nooch' or savoury yeast flakes. A good source of protein and vitamins, and widely available fortified with B12. Has a distinctive 'cheesy' flavour that makes it popular as a cheese substitute. Use with care as the flavour can be strong.

PLANT MILKS – milk substitutes made from soya beans, nuts, rice, oats and coconut, available in liquid and sometimes powdered form. Sweeteners are often added, so read cartons carefully and choose unsweetened where possible. Coconut milk is the richest and creamiest but tastes strongly of coconut. All recipes in this book use full-fat coconut milk. Almond milk is creamy, light and pleasant tasting. Soya milk is best for making buttermilk or yoghurt.

SEITAN – a form of wheat gluten often used as a meat substitute.

SUGAR – in some parts of the world, refined sugar is filtered through animal bone char. Check with the manufacturer if this is a concern for you.

TEMPEH – a traditional Indonesian ingredient made from soya beans, usually available in blocks or slices.

TOFU – made from soya milk mixed with a natural enzyme to produce soya curds, which are pressed to make silken (very creamy) through to extra firm (more solid and granular) tofu.

Firm tofu should be pressed before cooking: wrap a block in layers of paper towel, put between 2 chopping boards and put a heavy object on top. Leave for 20 minutes.

Silken tofu is softer than firm tofu and often used to make sour cream, mayonnaise, cheesecake and smoothies.

XANTHAN GUM – a thickening agent useful for dressings and sauces as an alternative to gelatine.

how to veganise a recipe

+ + +

Many non-vegan food products are available in vegan form including milk, cheese, yoghurt, butter and margarine, egg replacers, chocolate, ice cream and meat-style products. Quite often, it's simply a question of replacing a non-vegan ingredient with a vegan version.

The following table provides a rough guide for veganising non-vegan recipes.

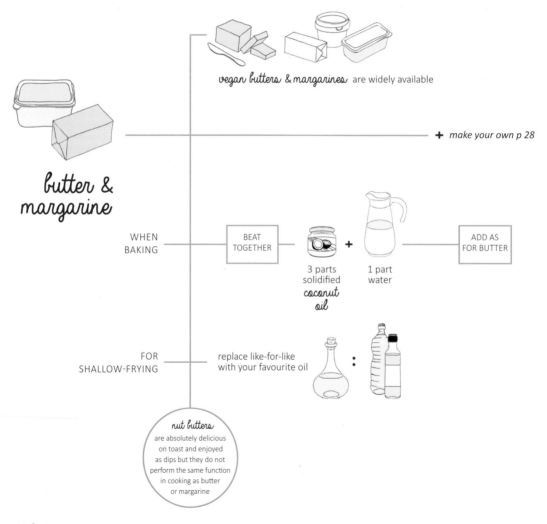

vegan butters & margarines are widely available

+ *make your own p 28*

butter & margarine

WHEN BAKING — BEAT TOGETHER — 3 parts solidified *coconut oil* + 1 part water — ADD AS FOR BUTTER

FOR SHALLOW-FRYING — replace like-for-like with your favourite oil

nut butters are absolutely delicious on toast and enjoyed as dips but they do not perform the same function in cooking as butter or margarine

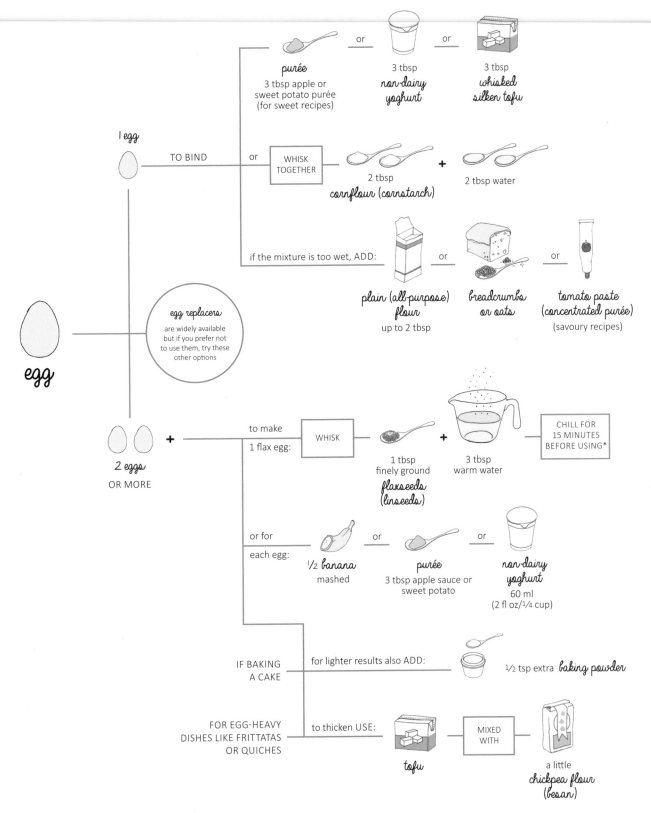

egg

1 egg

TO BIND — or —

purée
3 tbsp apple or
sweet potato purée
(for sweet recipes)

or

3 tbsp
*non-dairy
yoghurt*

or

3 tbsp
*whisked
silken tofu*

WHISK
TOGETHER

2 tbsp
cornflour (cornstarch)

+

2 tbsp water

if the mixture is too wet, ADD:

*plain (all-purpose)
flour*
up to 2 tbsp

or

*breadcrumbs
or oats*

or

*tomato paste
(concentrated purée)*
(savoury recipes)

egg replacers
are widely available
but if you prefer not
to use them, try these
other options

2 eggs
OR MORE

+

to make
1 flax egg:

WHISK

1 tbsp
finely ground
*flaxseeds
(linseeds)*

+

3 tbsp
warm water

CHILL FOR
15 MINUTES
BEFORE USING*

or for

each egg:

½ *banana*
mashed

or

purée
3 tbsp apple sauce or
sweet potato

or

*non-dairy
yoghurt*
60 ml
(2 fl oz/¼ cup)

IF BAKING
A CAKE

for lighter results also ADD:

½ tsp extra *baking powder*

FOR EGG-HEAVY
DISHES LIKE FRITTATAS
OR QUICHES

to thicken USE:

tofu

MIXED
WITH

a little
*chickpea flour
(besan)*

*The mixture should have the viscous consistency of eggs.
Flaxseeds lend a slightly nutty flavour to the recipe.

+ + +

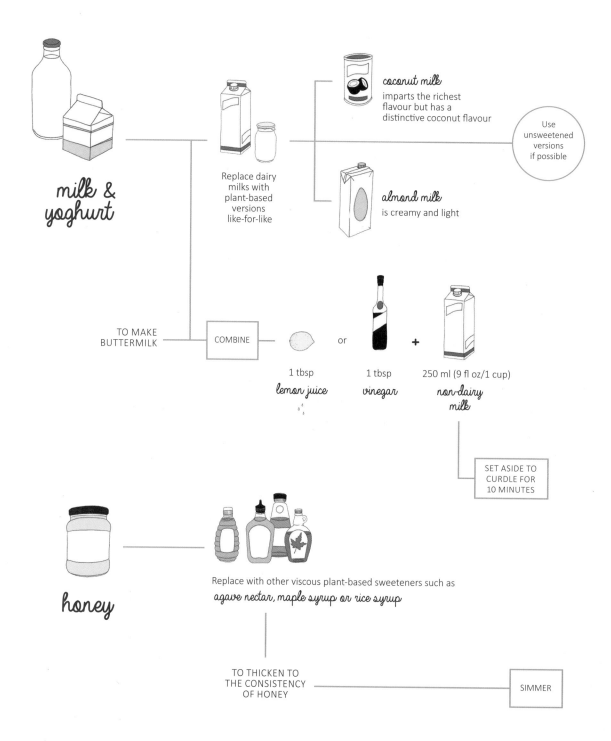

milk & yoghurt

Replace dairy milks with plant-based versions like-for-like

coconut milk
imparts the richest flavour but has a distinctive coconut flavour

almond milk
is creamy and light

Use unsweetened versions if possible

TO MAKE BUTTERMILK

COMBINE

1 tbsp
lemon juice

or

1 tbsp
vinegar

+

250 ml (9 fl oz/1 cup)
non-dairy milk

SET ASIDE TO CURDLE FOR 10 MINUTES

honey

Replace with other viscous plant-based sweeteners such as
agave nectar, maple syrup or rice syrup

TO THICKEN TO THE CONSISTENCY OF HONEY

SIMMER

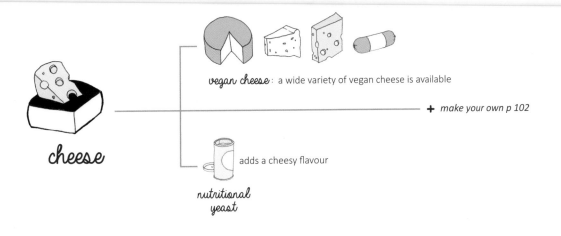

cheese

vegan cheese : a wide variety of vegan cheese is available

+ *make your own p 102*

adds a cheesy flavour

nutritional yeast

cream

vegan creams are widely available

+ *make your own p 26*

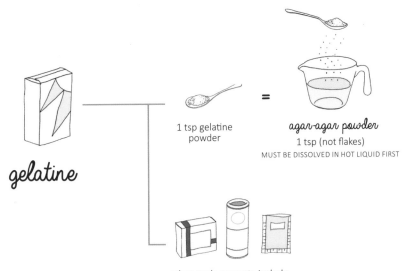

gelatine

1 tsp gelatine powder

=

agar-agar powder
1 tsp (not flakes)
MUST BE DISSOLVED IN HOT LIQUID FIRST

other replacements include
fruit pectin, carrageenan & xanthan gum

CHAPTER 1

basics

+ + +

HOW TO MAKE

milk

+++ +++

These non-dairy milks are delicious. Add them to smoothies, porridge, breakfast cereals, baked goods and soups, or just drink them! They can taste strongly of their core ingredient or sometimes a little bland, so improve the flavour by adding vanilla extract and/or agave nectar, maple or rice syrup, or dates (added to the blender before blitzing). I always add a pinch of good-quality sea salt flakes to enhance the flavour, but this isn't necessary.

The milk keeps well in the fridge for a couple of days and it's normal for it to separate, so just whisk before serving.

NUT MILK

Soak skinless raw almonds, cashew nuts, hazelnuts, Brazil nuts or macadamia nuts in water for 8–24 hours to plump up and soften. Drain, rinse and replenish the water once or twice during soaking. Blitz together 1 part soaked nuts to 2 parts water until very smooth and creamy – at least 2 minutes on full power. To make really smooth nut milk, strain through a piece of muslin, a nut bag or a clean piece of cut-off tights and squeeze out the milk. Dilute to taste.

250 ml (9 fl oz/1 cup) nuts yields about 700 ml (24 fl oz) milk.

SEED MILK

Soak raw hemp, sunflower, pumpkin or sesame seeds in water for at least 4 hours. Drain and rinse well. Blitz together 1 part soaked seeds to 3 or 4 parts water, depending on how thick you like your seed milk, until very smooth and creamy – at least 2 minutes on full power. To make really smooth seed milk, strain through a piece of muslin, a nut bag or a clean piece of cut-off tights and squeeze out the milk.

250 ml (9 fl oz/1 cup) seeds yields 650–800 ml (22½–28 fl oz) milk.

OAT MILK

Rinse 100 g (3½ oz/1 cup) rolled (porridge) oats in cold water, cover with just-boiled water and leave to soak for 20 minutes. Alternatively, soak overnight in cold water. Drain, rinse and transfer to a blender. Add 750 ml (26 fl oz/3 cups) cold water and blitz until smooth. To make really smooth oat milk, strain through a piece of muslin, a nut bag or a clean piece of cut-off tights and squeeze out the milk. Return the milk to a clean blender, blitz and strain again. Repeat if necessary for ultra-smooth milk.

Makes about 650 ml (22½ fl oz).

RICE MILK

Toast 60 g (2¼ oz) brown or white rice (brown produces more flavour) in a dry frying pan until fragrant and starting to brown. Cook according to your usual method until tender. Drain off any water and transfer to a blender with 650 ml (22½ fl oz) cold water. Blitz on high power until smooth and creamy. Push through a fine sieve to remove any stray rice grains and add more water if too thick.

Makes about 600 ml (21 fl oz).

SOYA MILK

Cover 85 g (3 oz) dried soya beans in 600 ml (21 fl oz) boiling water. Leave to soak for 12 hours, changing the water (cold water is fine) at least once. Drain, rinse and transfer to a blender. Add 500 ml (17 fl oz/2 cups) cold water and blitz until smooth. Strain through a piece of muslin, a nut bag or a clean piece of cut-off tights and squeeze out the milk. Blitz again until completely smooth. Transfer to a pan and gently simmer for 20 minutes, stirring occasionally. Add 1 teaspoon vanilla extract and 1 teaspoon caster (superfine) sugar and leave to cool.

Makes about 500 ml (17 fl oz/2 cups).

CONDENSED MILK

In a heavy pan, combine 1 litre (35 fl oz/4 cups) non-dairy milk with 80 g (2¾ oz) caster (superfine) sugar and a pinch of fine sea salt flakes. Very gently simmer, stirring frequently, until reduced to about 350 ml (12 fl oz). This could take 1 hour. Stir in 1 teaspoon vanilla extract.

Makes about 350 ml (12 fl oz).

HOW TO
MAKE

yoghurt

+++ +++

MAKES: 1 litre (35 fl oz/4 cups)
PREPARATION: 5 minutes,
plus up to 6 hours to incubate
COOKING: about 5 minutes

1 litre (35 fl oz/4 cups) soya milk
2 teaspoons agar-agar powder
4 g probiotic powder
Flavourings of choice (optional): sweeteners,
vanilla, cocoa powder, fruit purée and spices
like cinnamon or nutmeg

In a medium pan, bring the soya milk to the boil, then whisk in the agar-agar powder. Cook, whisking constantly to prevent the milk sticking to the bottom of the pan, for 3 minutes. Remove from the heat and set aside until the milk is cool enough to dip your finger into without burning. Whisk in the probiotic powder.

If you have a yoghurt maker, transfer the milk mixture to the appropriate jars and make the yoghurt according to the machine instructions.

+ + +

It's easy to make yoghurt and you don't need any fancy equipment, although by all means use a yoghurt maker if you have one. Just put in the oven with the oven light switched on: the yoghurt will take about 6 hours to incubate but the results are impressive, especially if you add your favourite flavourings.

If you don't have a yoghurt maker, transfer the mixture to clean jars, cover with clean tea towels (dish towels) and set on a baking tray. Switch on the oven light (don't turn the oven on!) and put the tray inside. Leave the jars inside until the mixture has turned thick and tastes tangy. This could take up to 6 hours, depending on your oven.

Add your favourite flavourings (if using). The yoghurt will keep in the fridge, covered, for 3 days.

cream

+++ +++

These cream replacements are lovely in sweet or savoury
recipes. The cashew cream is more versatile, as coconut cream
has quite a strong coconut flavour, but both are delicious.

CASHEW CREAM

Soak 100 g (3½ oz) raw cashew nuts in water for
at least 4 hours, then rinse well. Put in a blender
with 100 ml (3½ fl oz) cold water and blitz on full
power until completely smooth and creamy – at least
2 minutes. Add water for a thinner consistency.

Add salt, lemon juice and/or vegetable stock to taste
to smooth out the cashew flavour when using in
savoury dishes, or add vanilla extract, agave nectar,
rice syrup or maple syrup for sweet dishes. Will keep
in the fridge, covered, for a few days.

COCONUT CREAM

Tins of full-fat authentic Thai coconut milk work best for this, as they have the thickest layer of cream at the top. Chill the tin for a couple of hours before use, or put in the freezer for 30 minutes, then open without shaking.

Scoop out the layer of cream and beat with electric beaters until thick and creamy. Chill until ready to use. Add sweeteners such as vanilla extract, agave nectar, rice syrup or maple syrup for sweet dishes. Will keep in the fridge, covered, for a few days.

butter

+++ +++

MAKES: about 425 g (15 oz)
PREPARATION: 10 minutes
COOKING: none, once you have
melted the coconut oil

1 teaspoon soya lecithin granules
150 ml (5 fl oz) soya milk
1 tablespoon soya milk powder
1 teaspoon fine sea salt
140 ml sunflower oil
½ teaspoon xanthan gum
2 teaspoons nutritional yeast
200 ml (7 fl oz) refined coconut oil, melted

Grind the soya lecithin granules very finely in a
mortar or spice grinder.

Transfer to a food processor (it's difficult to make
this work well in a blender) and add all the remaining
ingredients except the coconut oil. Blitz until
well combined.

+ + +

Non-dairy butter is widely available in shops but it's also simple to make from scratch. This version is versatile enough to use as a like-for-like replacement for butter in most recipes, particularly pastry, cakes and buttercream icing. It also melts nicely on toast. It's not really suitable for frying. Soya lecithin granules, widely available from health food shops, are often used as an emulsifying agent.

With the motor running, gradually pour in the coconut oil. The mixture will thicken almost immediately.

Scrape into an airtight plastic container or roll up in baking paper and chill in the fridge to firm up. Keeps well, covered, for about 1 week.

mayonnaise

+++ +++

MAKES: about 200 ml (7 fl oz)
PREPARATION: 5 minutes
COOKING: none

120 g (4¼ oz) silken tofu
1 tablespoon lemon juice, or more to taste
1 teaspoon dijon mustard
¼ teaspoon sea salt flakes, or more to taste
¼ teaspoon xanthan gum (optional)
40 ml (1¼ fl oz) mild olive oil
50 ml (2½ tbsp) vegetable oil

Put the tofu, lemon juice, mustard, salt and xanthan gum (if using) in a blender.

Blitz the mixture until the ingredients are well combined and creamy.

+ + +

You can slip this past your non-vegan friends and they won't be able
to tell it apart from egg-based mayo as it looks and tastes so good.
Be sure to use silken tofu and not firm tofu. I've added xanthan gum to
make the mayo really thick and creamy, but it's not absolutely necessary.
Add flavourings like herbs or minced garlic, if you like.

Whisk together the 2 oils. With the blender running,
slowly drizzle in the oil mixture until thick and
emulsified. Season to taste with salt and more
lemon juice.

Transfer to an airtight container. The mayonnaise
will keep in the fridge, covered, for a few days.

HOW TO
MAKE

pasta

SERVES: 4 as a starter or 2 as a generous main
PREPARATION: 40 minutes, plus 45 minutes resting
COOKING: 3 minutes

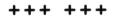

150 g (5½ oz) 00 flour, plus extra for dusting
1 pinch salt
1 teaspoon olive oil
80 ml (2½ fl oz/⅓ cup) freshly boiled water

Many people believe making pasta is too much bother, but this is simple and incredibly satisfying. It does require a little time to roll out the dough, but on the other hand it only takes 3 minutes to cook. Because the dough is eggless it is deliciously light and has a lovely *al dente* texture.

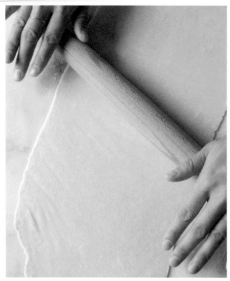

Combine the flour and salt in a bowl. Add the oil, then gradually add the boiled water, mixing with a fork until a dough forms. Knead on a floured work surface until smooth, about 10 minutes. Wrap in plastic wrap and rest for 45 minutes.

Roll out the dough to a thickness of 1–2 mm (1/32–1/16 inch) using a pasta machine or a rolling pin. If using a rolling pin, work with half the dough at a time, keeping the unused dough wrapped in plastic wrap.

Using a sharp knife or pizza cutter, cut the dough into long strips as wide or as narrow as you prefer.

Make little nests of pasta, sprinkle with flour and set aside on a flour-dusted tray until needed. The pasta will take about 3 minutes to cook in boiling salted water.

vegetable stock

MAKES: about 1.5 litres (52 fl oz/6 cups)
PREPARATION: 10 minutes
COOKING: 1 hour 5 minutes

+++ +++

2 tablespoons olive oil
2 onions, coarsely chopped
3 carrots, coarsely chopped
4 celery stalks and leaves, coarsely chopped
3 garlic cloves, bruised with the side of a knife
good optional extras to throw in:
coarsely chopped leeks, fennel,
tomatoes and fresh mushrooms
1 handful dried porcini or shiitake
mushrooms (optional)
1 handful fresh thyme sprigs
3 bay leaves
1 bunch flat-leaf (Italian) parsley
sea salt flakes
black peppercorns

There's nothing wrong with using good-quality stock (bouillon) cubes or stock (bouillon) powder, but home-made vegetable stock is hard to beat. It has a fresher flavour than shop-bought stock, which is often too salty and doesn't necessarily taste of vegetables. This is also very simple to make – quicker than meat-based stocks – and a terrific way to use odds and ends in the salad drawer that have passed their prime. The more veg you have in the pot the better.

Heat the oil in a large pan and add the vegetables, garlic and any optional extras. Don't add the porcini or shiitake mushrooms, herbs or seasoning just yet. Sweat over a medium heat for 5 minutes, or until the vegetables start releasing their juices.

Pour in enough cold water to cover the vegetables by 5 cm (2 inches) – you should be able to stir them around easily – then add the porcini or shiitake, the herbs and seasonings.

When the pot starts to bubble, reduce the heat to medium–low and cook gently for at least 1 hour. The longer you cook the stock the more intense the flavour will be. Stir now and then to circulate the vegetables. Strain.

Use immediately or leave to cool, then freeze in bags, plastic lidded containers or ice cube trays. If you have a shortage of freezer space, reduce the stock down further before freezing. Defrost when needed, then dilute with water. Store frozen for 2–3 months.

basic pastry

MAKES: 2 x 20 cm (8 inch) galettes or quiches, or 1 x 20 cm (8 inch) pie with a pastry lid
PREPARATION: 10 minutes, plus 30 minutes chilling
COOKING: varies according to the topping or filling

200 g (7 oz/1⅓ cups) plain (all-purpose) flour,
plus extra for dusting
1 pinch salt
1 tablespoon caster (superfine) sugar (only if
making sweet pastry)
75 g non-dairy butter, chilled
45–70 ml (1½–2¼ fl oz) iced water

This is a very versatile pastry as it can be used for both sweet and savoury recipes. Chilling the dough is important to give the gluten time to relax, making it easier to roll out.

Whisk together the flour, salt and sugar (if making sweet pastry). Cut the butter into small dice and rub into the flour to make a breadcrumb consistency.

Using a blunt knife, gradually mix in the water to make a dough. Tip out onto a lightly floured work surface, bring the mixture together and lightly knead. Divide into 2 pieces, shape into discs and wrap individually in baking paper. Chill for 30 minutes.

Roll out the dough between 2 sheets of lightly floured baking paper – 3 mm (⅛ inch) thick is perfect – and carefully peel back the top layer of paper. Work with one piece of dough at a time, leaving the rest in the fridge until ready to roll.

If lining a pastry tin, loosely roll the pastry around the rolling pin and drape over the tin. Gently press the pastry into the tin and fill according to recipe instructions. If making a galette, leave the pastry on its paper and add the topping. Slide the paper and pastry onto a baking tray to cook.

how to make basic pastry 37

CHAPTER 2

brunch

+++

Just put all the ingredients in the blender for these smoothies and blitz until smooth. These are quite thick smoothies so add a splash of water or more milk if you prefer a thinner consistency.

smoothies

+++ +++

CHOCOLATE (right)

185 ml (6 fl oz/¾ cup) coconut milk
½ banana
1 tablespoon maple syrup
20 g (¾ oz) chopped dates
1 pinch salt
½ tablespoon cocoa powder

MATCHA (left)

1 teaspoon Matcha powder
(not green tea)
½ apple, cored and chopped
20 g (¾ oz) trimmed silverbeet
(Swiss chard) or baby English spinach
10 mint leaves
¼ banana
½ pear, cored
100 ml (3½ fl oz) water

GREEN (left)

¼ cucumber, peeled
60 g (2¼ oz) fennel bulb, sliced
25 g (1 oz/½ cup) baby English
spinach leaves
½ apple, cored and chopped
80 ml (2½ fl oz/⅓ cup) thin
pumpkin seed milk or water

BEETROOT (above)

50 g (1¾ oz) peeled and chopped
raw beetroot (beets)
½ apple, cored and chopped
¼ cucumber, peeled and chopped
1 tablespoon lemon juice
1 small handful chopped flat-leaf
(Italian) parsley
80 ml (2½ fl oz/⅓ cup) water

TUTTI FRUITI (above)

70 g (2½ oz) watermelon, chopped
100 g (3½ oz) chopped mango
1 small peach, peeled and chopped
2 tablespoons coconut milk

BERRY GOOD (right)

150 g (5½ oz) blueberries
200 ml (7 fl oz) almond milk
8 mint leaves
1 tablespoon goji berries
1 generous squeeze lime juice

quinoa bircher breakfast bowl

WITH CARAMELISED BANANAS & COCONUT YOGHURT

This bowl of tasty goodness will power you through the day.
The amount of milk you need for soaking will vary according to the thickness
of your milk. Use as much as you need to achieve quite a wet mixture.

SERVES: 4–6
PREPARATION: 10 minutes, plus overnight soaking
COOKING: 3 minutes

80 g (2¾ oz) rolled (porridge) oats
100 g (3½ oz/½ cup) quinoa flakes
40 g (1½ oz) mixed seeds like chia, flax,
sunflower and pumpkin
900 ml (30½ fl oz) almond milk,
plus more if needed
3 tablespoons agave nectar or maple syrup
2 apples, cored and grated
½ banana for each serving
1 teaspoon each per serve coconut oil,
for frying

dried fruit such as goji berries, cherries or
cranberries, or chopped apricots, dates or figs
dairy-free yoghurt (preferably coconut),
to serve

OPTIONAL EXTRAS
toasted coconut or almond flakes, pecans or
Brazil nuts, fresh berries

Combine the oats, quinoa flakes, seeds, milk,
agave or maple syrup and apple, and stir to
combine. Put in an airtight container, transfer
to the fridge and leave to plump up for several
hours, ideally overnight.

When almost ready to serve, cut the bananas
into thick slices. Heat the coconut oil in a frying
pan and add the banana. Cook over a medium–
high heat for 90 seconds each to caramelise.

Serve the oats and quinoa mixture topped with
the caramelised bananas, a sprinkling of dried
fruit, a splodge of yoghurt and any optional extras
you fancy.

baked berry porridge

WITH COCONUT

If you need to make breakfast or brunch for a crowd, this is ideal: creamy porridge exploding with berry flavour, without the hassle of stirring a pot.

SERVES: 6
PREPARATION: 10 minutes
COOKING: 45 minutes, plus 5 minutes cooling

vegetable oil, for brushing
150 g (5½ oz/1½ cups) rolled (porridge) oats
80 g (2¾ oz) wholemeal (whole-wheat) flour
40 g (1½ oz) desiccated (shredded) coconut
3 teaspoons ground cinnamon
1 teaspoon ground ginger
½ teaspoon fine sea salt
625 ml (21½ fl oz/2½ cups) rice milk

3 tablespoons agave nectar
2 tablespoons berry coulis or 1 tablespoon berry jam mixed with 2 tablespoons water
2 teaspoons vanilla extract
1 banana
175 g (6 oz) fresh raspberries
100 g (3½ oz/¾ cup) fresh blackberries
2 tablespoons caster (superfine) sugar

Heat the oven to 180°C (350°F/Gas 4). Lightly brush a 2 litre (70 fl oz/8 cup) baking dish with oil.

In a mixing bowl, whisk together the oats, flour, coconut, 2 teaspoons of the cinnamon, the ginger and salt. Add the milk, agave, berry coulis and vanilla. Stir to combine. Chop the banana and gently fold in, along with most of the raspberries.

Pour into the prepared baking dish and push the blackberries and the remaining raspberries into the oat mixture. Combine the caster sugar and remaining cinnamon and sprinkle over the top. Bake for 45 minutes: when done the top should be slightly golden and the porridge creamy. Leave to stand for 5 minutes, then serve immediately.

coconut & banana breakfast squares

Making these scrumptious bars barely constitutes cooking. Blitz the ingredients, pop the baking tin in the oven and you've got a week's worth of breakfasts! A piece of fruit or a pot of yoghurt alongside makes for a terrific breakfast on the hoof.

MAKES: 16 squares
PREPARATION: 5 minutes
COOKING: 30 minutes

300 g (10½ oz) pitted dates
200 g (7 oz/2 cups) rolled (porridge) oats
60 g (2¼ oz) wholemeal (whole-wheat) flour
30 g (1 oz/⅓ cup) desiccated (shredded) coconut
80 g (2¾ oz) banana chips
1 teaspoon fine sea salt

1 teaspoon ground cinnamon
125 ml (4 fl oz/½ cup) mild olive oil
120 g (4¼ oz) agave nectar
2 ripe bananas, broken into pieces
2 tablespoons chia seeds (optional)

Heat the oven to 180°C (350°F/Gas 4). Line a 20 cm (8 inch) square baking tin with foil, letting the edges of the foil overhang the sides.

Put all the ingredients in a food processor and blitz to make a coarse but well combined batter. Scrape into the prepared tin and bake for 30 minutes. The top should be firm and slightly golden. Leave in the tin for a couple of minutes, then lift onto a wire rack to cool.

Cut into 16 squares. Eat warm or cold.

buckwheat & blueberry pancakes

WITH MAPLE CASHEW CREAM

Pancakes are always delicious but sometimes it's nice to ring some changes. Here the buckwheat flour imparts a rich, nutty and slightly sour taste, which marries well with the luscious cashew cream.

MAKES: 12 x 8 cm (3¼ inch) pancakes
PREPARATION: 10 minutes, once cashew cream is made
COOKING: 15 minutes

2–3 tablespoons maple syrup, plus extra for drizzling
250 ml (9 fl oz/1 cup) cashew cream (*see* p 26)
50 g (1¾ oz) buckwheat flour
50 g (1¾ oz/⅓ cup) plain (all-purpose) flour
½ teaspoon baking powder
1 tablespoon caster (superfine) sugar
1 pinch fine sea salt

200 ml (7 fl oz) non-dairy milk
½ teaspoon vanilla extract
½ teaspoon vegetable oil, plus more for frying
2 tablespoons mashed banana
100 g (3½ oz/⅔ cup) blueberries, plus extra to serve

Stir the maple syrup into the cashew cream and chill until ready to serve.

In a mixing bowl, whisk together the flours, baking powder, sugar and salt. In a jug, mix together the milk, vanilla, the vegetable oil and the mashed banana. Gradually whisk the wet ingredients into the dry to form a smooth batter. Fold in the blueberries.

Heat a large heavy frying pan and add a little oil. Wipe the oil over the base of the pan with a paper towel. When the pan is hot, drop in heaped tablespoons of the batter and cook over a medium–high heat for 1 minute, or until bubbles start to form on top. Flip and cook for about 30 seconds more. Repeat until the batter is used up, keeping the cooked pancakes warm.

Serve with a dollop of the chilled maple cashew cream, a drizzle of maple syrup and some extra blueberries.

fruit loaf

WITH APPLE BUTTER

Although this takes a little time to prepare, it's not onerous and is a great way to feed a crowd for brunch. The loaf is lovely served warm from the oven, or toasted and thickly spread with apple butter.

MAKES: 1 loaf
PREPARATION: 30 minutes, plus 1 hour 10 minutes proving
COOKING: 1 hour 20 minutes, plus cooling

500 g (1 lb 2 oz/3⅓ cups) plain (all-purpose) flour, plus extra for kneading
50 g (1¾ oz) caster (superfine) sugar
3 teaspoons mixed spice
7 g fast-action dried yeast
1 teaspoon vanilla extract
1 teaspoon almond extract
vegetable oil, for oiling
finely grated zest of 1 orange
225 g (8 oz) chopped dried fruit, such as apricots, dates, raisins or dried cherries

FOR THE APPLE BUTTER
750 g (1 lb 10 oz) apples
100 g (3½ oz) caster (superfine) sugar
juice of ½ lemon
½ teaspoon ground cinnamon
1 star anise

Whisk together the flour, sugar, mixed spice and yeast. Combine the vanilla and almond extract with 300 ml (10½ fl oz) water and gradually stir into the flour. Bring the mixture together into a soft dough and tip out onto a lightly oiled work surface. Knead for 10 minutes, adding more flour if too sticky. Put in an oiled bowl, cover with oiled plastic wrap and leave somewhere warm for 1 hour.

Meanwhile, peel, chop and core the apples and put in a heavy lidded pan with 125 ml (4 fl oz/½ cup) water. Simmer with the lid ajar for 20 minutes, adding a splash of water if necessary. Purée in a food processor. Pour purée into the pan and add the sugar, lemon juice, cinnamon and star anise. Cook over a very low heat for 1 hour, or until the purée is thick and deep brown. Discard the star anise.

Lightly oil a loaf (bar) tin and line the base with baking paper. Combine the orange zest and dried fruit. Turn the dough out onto a lightly oiled work surface, flatten with your knuckles and gradually knead in the dried fruit. Roll into a log shape, put in the loaf tin and cover with a clean tea towel (dish towel). Set aside for 10 minutes.

While the dough is proving, heat the oven to 200°C (400°F/Gas 6) and put a baking tin half-filled with water in the bottom of the oven. Bake the loaf on the middle shelf for 10 minutes, then reduce the heat to 170°C (325°F/Gas 3) and bake for a further 45 minutes. Leave in the tin for a few minutes then turn out onto a wire rack to cool. Slice and serve with the apple butter.

breakfast burritos

WITH REFRIED BEANS

Burritos are a perfect brunch dish as they're substantial but don't require much preparation or cooking. In fact, you can put the burrito components on the table and invite guests to assemble their own.

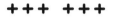

SERVES: 4
PREPARATION: 15 minutes
COOKING: 20 minutes

600 g (1 lb 5 oz) potatoes, peeled and diced small
2 tablespoons rapeseed or vegetable oil
1½ teaspoons smoked sweet paprika
160 g (5¾ oz) non-dairy cream cheese
finely grated zest and juice of 1 lime
sea salt flakes
freshly ground black pepper
3 tablespoons olive oil
2 garlic cloves, finely sliced

1 red chilli, seeded and finely sliced, or
1 chipotle in adobo, drained and finely sliced
4 tablespoons chopped coriander (cilantro) leaves and stalks, plus extra to serve
2 x 400 g (14 oz) tinned black beans or kidney beans, drained, liquid reserved
4 flour tortillas, to serve
2 ripe tomatoes, chopped small
chilli sauce, to serve (optional)

Heat the oven to 220°C (425°F/Gas 7). Toss the potatoes in the oil, sprinkle with the paprika and spread out in a single layer in a baking tray. Roast for 20 minutes, or until cooked and golden.

Meanwhile, combine the cream cheese with the lime zest and half the lime juice. Season with salt and pepper and chill until needed.

Heat the olive oil in a large frying pan and add the garlic, chilli or chipotle and the coriander. Stir-fry for a minute or so over a medium heat until aromatic and starting to colour. Add the beans, stir, and season with salt and pepper. Cook, stirring often, for about 5 minutes or until

the beans soften. Stir in a splash of water and mash with the back of a wooden spoon or potato masher. Keep mashing and adding liquid to achieve the desired consistency – some people like the beans creamy while others prefer some texture. Add the remaining lime juice and taste for seasoning as beans often need lots of salt.

To serve, spoon some of the potatoes and beans into the centre of a tortilla. Add some of the tomatoes, a spoonful of the cream cheese mixture, some coriander and chilli sauce (if using). Fold in the sides, roll up and repeat. Eat immediately.

scrambled tofu

WITH BLACK BEANS AND SPINACH

Delicious and hearty, this is a brunch dish where I don't notice the absence of eggs. The pickled chipotles add a lovely smoky punch of flavour, but replace with 2 tablespoons tomato sauce (ketchup) if you prefer.

SERVES: 4
PREPARATION: 10 minutes
COOKING: 15 minutes

400 g (14 oz) firm tofu, drained
3 tablespoons olive oil
1 white onion, finely chopped
1 garlic clove, crushed
1 small orange or red capsicum (pepper), cut into strips
1 teaspoon ground cumin
½ teaspoon turmeric
1 squeeze lemon juice

1 x 400 g (14 oz) tinned black beans, rinsed and drained
1 small handful of baby English spinach
1 tablespoon chopped chipotle in adobo (drained)
2 tablespoons nutritional yeast
2 tablespoons chopped coriander (cilantro)
chilli sauce, to taste (optional)

Dry the tofu with paper towels and break into bite-sized pieces. Set aside on paper towels. Heat 2 tablespoons of the oil in a frying pan and cook the onion over a medium heat until soft. Add the garlic, capsicum, cumin and turmeric and cook, stirring, until the capsicum is soft, about 2 minutes. Add a splash of water if the pan becomes dry.

Add the remaining oil and the tofu and cook over a medium heat for about 5 minutes. Gently turn over the tofu pieces as they cook but not too often as they need time to caramelise. When the tofu is golden, squeeze over the lemon juice and scrape up the crusty bits from the bottom of the pan. Add the beans, spinach and chipotles and sprinkle over the nutritional yeast. Toss the ingredients together and cook for about 2 minutes, or until the beans are warmed through and the nutritional yeast melted. Serve immediately, sprinkled with the coriander and a splash of chilli sauce (if using).

French toast

WITH BERRIES

Make sure you use lovely thick slices of bread here. If the bread is a little bit stale, all the better, as this will save you toasting it before frying.

MAKES: 4 pieces
PREPARATION: 5 minutes, plus a few minutes soaking
COOKING: 5 minutes

4 slices thick white bread
250 ml (9 fl oz/1 cup) coconut milk
90 ml (3 fl oz) unsweetened almond milk
2 tablespoons maple syrup, plus extra for drizzling
1 tablespoon plain (all-purpose) flour

½ teaspoon ground cinnamon
1 pinch salt
1–2 tablespoons coconut oil, for frying
mixed berries, to serve
sifted icing (confectioners') sugar, for dusting

Lightly toast the bread if fresh. Meanwhile, whisk together the milks, syrup, flour, cinnamon and salt. Arrange the bread in a single layer in a wide shallow dish and pour over the milk mixture. Turn to coat and set aside for a few minutes.

Melt the oil in a frying pan over a medium–high heat. Add the soaked bread slices and cook for a couple of minutes each side, or until golden. Serve immediately with berries, a drizzle of syrup and a dusting of icing sugar.

ricotta & avocado toasts

WITH CHILLI FLAKES

This is one of my favourite brunch dishes and is very quick to make. Just make sure your avocados are ripe and the bread is good quality. If serving a crowd, cook the toast in bulk under a grill, put the bowls of ricotta and avocado on the table and invite guests to assemble the toasts themselves.

MAKES: 4 slices
PREPARATION: 10 minutes, once the ricotta is made
COOKING: a few minutes for the toast

2 large ripe avocados
sea salt flakes
freshly ground black pepper
juice of 1 lime, plus extra to serve if needed
4 slices good-quality sourdough or country-style bread

olive oil, for brushing
1 quantity non-dairy ricotta (*see* p 102)
chilli flakes, for sprinkling
1 small handful basil leaves, torn

Peel and slice the avocados, season with salt and pepper and toss with the lime juice. Alternatively, cut the avocados in half, scoop the flesh into a bowl and mash with a fork. Add salt and pepper and lime juice to taste.

Heat a griddle pan until very hot and lightly brush the bread on both sides with oil. Griddle the bread until lightly charred on both sides.

To serve, spread the ricotta on the hot toast and top with the mashed avocado. Sprinkle with chilli flakes and basil leaves and squeeze over a little more lime juice if desired. Add salt and pepper to taste and serve immediately.

cheese & spinach muffins

WITH A PINCH OF PAPRIKA

Great for breakfast or brunch on the run, these savoury
muffins are quick and easy to put together.

MAKES: 12
PREPARATION: 15 minutes, once the flax egg is made
COOKING: 25 minutes

150 g (5½ oz/1⅓ cups) baby English spinach
200 g (7 oz/1⅓ cups) self-raising flour
3 tablespoons nutritional yeast
1 teaspoon mustard powder
1 teaspoon sweet smoked paprika
½ teaspoon fine sea salt

freshly ground black pepper
175 ml non-dairy milk
25 ml vegetable oil
1 flax egg (*see* p 17)
75 g non-dairy cheese, grated

Heat the oven to 190°C (375°F/Gas 5). Line a
12-hole muffin tin with paper cases.

Put the spinach in a pan, add a splash of water
and set over a medium–high heat. Stir until
wilted – it will only take a minute or so. Drain the
spinach, wrap in a clean tea towel (dish towel)
and squeeze out any excess water. Chop.

Mix the flour, 2 tablespoons of the nutritional
yeast, the mustard powder, paprika and salt and
pepper in a bowl. In another bowl, mix together
the milk, oil and the flax egg.

Mix the wet mixture into the dry – only just
enough to combine – then fold in the cheese
and spinach.

Spoon the mixture into the prepared paper cases.
Sprinkle with the remaining nutritional yeast and
bake for 20–25 minutes until firm to the touch
and golden. Best enjoyed warm.

eggs Benedict

Let's be honest: this isn't anything like the classic version made
with eggs and a buttery sauce. It is, however, a yummy
alternative and a terrific brunch dish.

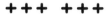

SERVES: 4
PREPARATION: 20 minutes, plus 30 minutes infusing and pressing
COOKING: 20 minutes

120 ml coconut milk
120 ml unsweetened soya milk
2 bay leaves
2 garlic cloves, peeled and bruised with the side of a knife
1 generous pinch saffron threads, crushed
1 tablespoon soy sauce
2 tablespoons agave nectar
3 drops liquid smoke* (optional)
2 tablespoons rapeseed oil
400 g (14 oz) firm tofu, pressed (*see* p 15) and sliced into 4 pieces

2 tablespoons refined coconut oil
1 tablespoon potato starch or cornflour (cornstarch)
2 teaspoons lemon juice, or more to taste
1/2 teaspoon white miso paste
sea salt flakes
white pepper
2 English muffins, split
2 tablespoons vegetable oil
1 large tomato, cut into 4 slices
4 slices vegan ham (optional)
2 tablespoons chopped chives

Combine the milks in a pan, add the bay leaves
and garlic and bring to the boil. Remove from the
heat and leave to infuse for 10 minutes.

Meanwhile, soak the crushed saffron threads
in 1 tablespoon hot water and set aside. Whisk
together the soy, agave, liquid smoke (if using)
and rapeseed oil. Arrange the tofu in a single layer
in a shallow bowl and pour over the soy mixture.
Turn to coat and then set aside.

When the milk has infused, discard the garlic
and bay leaves. Heat the coconut oil in a pan
and stir in the potato starch or cornflour until
amalgamated. Over a medium heat, gradually
whisk in the hot milk until thick and creamy. Add
the saffron and its soaking liquid and the lemon

juice. Mix the miso paste with a splash of warm
water and add this too. Season with salt and
pepper, stir, then set aside to keep warm.

Toast the muffins. Meanwhile, heat the vegetable
oil in a large frying pan, add the tofu (shaking off
excess marinade) and the tomato slices. Fry the
tofu on both sides until golden. Flip the tomatoes
now and then.

To serve, top each muffin-half with a slice of
ham (if using), tomato and tofu. Spoon over
some of the sauce and sprinkle with chives.
Serve immediately.

*A smoky flavouring available at some supermarkets
and online.

CHAPTER 3

starters & light bites

+ + +

mushroom pâté

This is delicious served with thinly sliced toast and cornichons on the side.

+++ +++

MAKES: 2 x 200 ml (7 fl oz) ramekins
PREPARATION: 10 minutes
COOKING: 20 minutes

3 tablespoons olive oil
500 g (1 lb 2 oz) mixed mushrooms, chopped
1 onion, finely chopped
1 large garlic clove, minced
2 tablespoons chopped thyme

1 squeeze lemon juice, plus extra to taste
60 ml (2 fl oz/¼ cup) sweet Marsala or port
4 tablespoons non-dairy sour cream
sea salt flakes
freshly ground black pepper

Heat the oil in a frying pan, add the mushrooms, onion, garlic and thyme and gently cook for about 15 minutes, or until soft. Add the squeeze of lemon juice and the Marsala or port and fry for 1 minute more. Drain off any excess liquid and leave to cool for 5 minutes.

Transfer the mushrooms to a blender, add the sour cream and salt and pepper and blitz until smooth. Taste for seasoning, adding more salt and pepper or lemon juice if needed. Scrape into ramekins and chill to set a little before serving.

Mediterranean terrine

Sometimes it's worth making a little extra effort to cook something for a special occasion, and this is a beautiful and tasty option. It's crucial to season generously with salt and pepper between each of the layers.

SERVES: 6–8
PREPARATION: 30 minutes
COOKING: about 1 hour, plus 2 hours 30 minutes chilling and cooling

1 large eggplant (aubergine)
fine sea salt, for sprinkling
2 tablespoons olive oil, plus extra for brushing and oiling
3 zucchini (courgettes), thinly sliced lengthways
3 yellow capsicums (peppers), quartered and seeded
2 large red onions, sliced into rings
1 garlic clove, finely chopped
2 tablespoons tomato paste (concentrated purée)

2 tablespoons balsamic vinegar
2 teaspoons caster (superfine) sugar
sea salt flakes
freshly ground black pepper
455 ml (16 fl oz) tomato passata (puréed tomatoes)
1 tablespoon agar-agar powder
250 g (9 oz) marinated red capsicum (pepper) (drained weight)
basil leaves, to serve

Cut the eggplant lengthways into 1 cm (½ inch) slices, sprinkle with fine sea salt and put in a colander set over a bowl for 20 minutes. Pat dry.

Meanwhile, set a griddle pan over a high heat, lightly brush with oil and cook the zucchinis until tender and charred. Set aside. Brush the griddle with more oil and cook the yellow capsicums in the same way, setting them aside separately to the zucchini. Repeat with the eggplant.

For the onion layer, heat the olive oil in a pan and cook the onions for 5 minutes, or until very soft. Add the garlic and cook for 3 minutes more. Stir in the tomato paste, vinegar and 1 teaspoon of the sugar. Cook for a further 3 minutes. Season with salt and pepper. Set aside.

For the passata layer, simmer the passata, the remaining sugar and 100 ml (3½ fl oz) water in

a small pan for 5 minutes. Add the agar-agar and simmer for 3 minutes more, stirring. Set aside.

To assemble, lightly oil a 24 x 12 cm (9½ x 4½ inch) loaf (bar) tin and line with plastic wrap, letting it overhang the sides. Spread a thin layer of passata mixture over the base. Layer the zucchini on top and season with salt and pepper. Add more passata, then the eggplant slices. Repeat with the yellow capsicum and onions, seasoning and adding some of the passata mixture in between. Finish with the red capsicum, then gently press to compact the vegetables. Pour over the remaining passata. Cool for 30 minutes, then chill for at least 2 hours.

When ready to serve, invert the tin onto a serving plate or board, lift off the tin and carefully peel away the plastic wrap. Slice and scatter with basil leaves to serve. Delicious served with non-dairy sour cream and country-style bread.

pizzettes

WITH MOZZARELLA & ONION RELISH

There may seem to be an excessive number of onions in this dish, but they cook right down into a sweet and gorgeous relish. These make a brilliant starter or light meal, served with a heap of bitter dressed leaves to complement the sweetness of the onion.

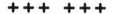

MAKES: 6 x 15 cm (6 inch) pizzettes
PREPARATION: 20 minutes
COOKING: 40 minutes

190 g (6¾ oz) plain (all-purpose) flour, plus extra for dusting
½ teaspoon fine sea salt
3.5 g fast-action dried yeast
1 teaspoon caster (superfine) sugar
60 ml (2 fl oz/¼ cup) olive oil, plus extra for oiling and drizzling
110 ml warm water

1.5 kg (3 lb 5 oz) onions, sliced
4 garlic cloves, sliced
1 tablespoon soft light brown sugar
3 tablespoons balsamic vinegar
sea salt flakes
freshly ground black pepper
12 heaped tablespoons grated non-dairy mozzarella or other cheese

In a mixing bowl, whisk together the flour, salt, yeast and caster sugar. Make a well in the centre and pour in 1 tablespoon of the olive oil and the warm water. Bring the mixture together with your hands, tip out onto a lightly oiled work surface and knead until smooth and elastic, about 10 minutes. Break into 6 equal pieces, roll into balls and put on a baking tray. Cover with a clean damp tea towel (dish towel) and set aside.

Heat the remaining olive oil in a large pan, add the onions and garlic and stir well to coat. Cook over a medium heat until soft, sticky and golden, about

20 minutes. Stir in the soft light brown sugar and vinegar and season with salt and pepper. Cook, stirring for a few minutes more. Taste for seasoning.

Heat the oven to 220°C (425°F/Gas 7). On a lightly floured work surface, roll out the dough balls into 15 cm (6 inch) discs and arrange on 1 large or 2 small baking trays. Divide the onion mixture between the discs, spreading it up to the edges. Top with grated mozzarella and drizzle with olive oil. Bake for about 10–12 minutes, or until the base is crisp and golden and the top bubbling.

witlof cups

WITH WALNUT TABOULEH

These chic little bites make perfect finger food as Mother Nature has provided her own edible crockery. The key to the success of this tabouleh is to chop everything very finely so the flavours really intermingle.

MAKES: about 16 cups
PREPARATION: 30 minutes
COOKING: none

100 g (3½ oz) walnuts
sea salt flakes
1 handful flat-leaf (Italian) parsley, finely chopped
1 handful mint, finely chopped
50 g (1¾ oz/⅓ cup) finely chopped red onion
30 g (1 oz) dried goji berries or chopped dried cranberries
1 red apple

freshly ground black pepper
about 16 witlof (chicory) leaves

FOR THE DRESSING
60 ml (2 fl oz/¼ cup) lemon juice
125 ml (4 fl oz/½ cup) olive oil
2 teaspoons agave nectar, or more to taste
sea salt flakes
freshly ground black pepper

Toast the walnuts in a dry frying pan until fragrant, about 3 minutes. Transfer to a mortar, add a pinch of salt and pound to a coarse rubble. Set aside.

Whisk together the dressing ingredients.

Combine the parsley, mint, onion, dried fruit and walnuts in a salad bowl. Core and dice the apple very small and add to the bowl. Add the dressing a tablespoonful at a time, tossing between each addition. Stop when everything is coated – you might not need it all. Taste for seasoning and add more salt and pepper if necessary.

Arrange the witlof leaves on a platter and serve with 1 or 2 teaspoons of the tabouleh spooned into each one.

crudités

WITH WHIPPED GARLIC DIP

No question, this is super simple to put together. But if you choose your veggies artfully – no limp celery stalks please – it's an impressive and tasty starter or pre-dinner plate of nibbles. Beware: it is very garlicky.

MAKES: about 250 ml (9 fl oz/1 cup)
PREPARATION: 5 minutes
COOKING: none

FOR THE DIP
1 x 400 g (14 oz) tinned butterbeans, drained and rinsed
100 ml (3½ fl oz) mild extra virgin olive oil
3 garlic cloves
½ teaspoon fine sea salt
finely grated zest and juice of ½ lemon
freshly ground black pepper

TO SERVE
mixed raw vegetables such as broccolini, baby carrots, breakfast radishes, sliced red capsicum (pepper), snow peas (mangetout), cos (romaine) hearts, green beans, cherry tomatoes, cucumber (sliced lengthways) and boiled kipfler (fingerling) potatoes
good-quality sea salt flakes, for dipping (optional)

To make the dip, put all the ingredients in a blender and blitz until smooth. You will need to scrape down the sides of the bowl with a spatula a couple of times.

Serve the dip in a bowl alongside a platter of the vegetables, with a tiny bowl of sea salt flakes for dipping (if using).

crispy polenta bites

WITH GREEN TAPENADE

Making tasty finger food for a crowd can be headache-inducing but this recipe is delicious and much of it can be prepared in advance. Make the polenta and tapenade ahead of time and it will take just 10 minutes or so to cut and fry the squares.

MAKES: 25
PREPARATION: 10 minutes
COOKING: 15 minutes, plus 3 hours cooling and chilling

FOR THE POLENTA
750 ml (26 fl oz/3 cups) hot vegetable stock
140 g (5 oz) instant polenta (cornmeal)
¼ teaspoon fine sea salt
freshly ground black pepper
1 teaspoon dried oregano
3 tablespoons potato starch or cornflour (cornstarch), for dusting
3 tablespoons olive oil, for frying

FOR THE TAPENADE
175 g (6 oz) pitted green olives
1 garlic clove
2 tablespoons capers, rinsed
90 ml (3 fl oz) olive oil, plus extra for brushing
finely grated zest of ½ lemon
2 teaspoons lemon juice
1 teaspoon chopped thyme leaves
freshly ground black pepper

Line a 20 cm (8 inch) square baking tray with foil, letting it overhang the sides.

To make the polenta, combine the stock, polenta and salt and pepper in a pan and bring to the boil over a medium–high heat. Reduce the heat to medium and stir constantly until very thick, about 5 minutes. Stir in the oregano. Pour into the prepared baking tray and smooth the top with a spatula. Leave to cool, then transfer to the fridge to firm up for at least 2 hours.

Meanwhile, make the tapenade. Put all the ingredients in a food processor and blitz until well combined – you want a slightly chunky texture. Taste for seasoning and set aside.

When the polenta is firm and you're ready to serve, lift it out of the baking tray and put on a chopping board. Cut into 4 cm (1½ inch) squares with a sharp knife. Spread the potato starch or cornflour out on a plate. Toss the polenta squares in the flour, shaking off any excess.

Heat the olive oil in a frying pan and fry the squares over a medium–high heat for about 4 minutes each side, or until golden.

Transfer to paper towels. To serve, arrange the polenta squares on a platter and top with a spoonful of tapenade. Best served hot.

caraway seed pastries

WITH MANGO CHILLI JAM

These Indian-inspired bites are a bit naughty (being deep-fried) but are crumbly, flaky and utterly delicious. On the off chance you don't eat them all in one sitting, store them in an airtight container for a couple of days.

MAKES: 30 pastries with jam left over
PREPARATION: 20 minutes
COOKING: 50 minutes

FOR THE JAM
2 tablespoons vegetable oil
2 red onions, chopped
2 garlic cloves, crushed
2 red chillies, halved, seeded and finely sliced
6 cardamom pods, crushed with the side of a knife
2 scant teaspoons garam masala
60 ml (2 fl oz/1/4 cup) tablespoon red wine vinegar
400 g (14 oz) mango flesh (about 2 large mangoes), chopped

60 ml (2 fl oz/1/4 cup) golden syrup (light treacle)
1/2 teaspoon fine sea salt

FOR THE PASTRIES
2 teaspoons caraway seeds
225 g (8 oz) plain (all-purpose) flour
1/2 teaspoon salt
80 ml (21/2 fl oz/1/3 cup) warm vegetable oil, plus extra for deep-frying
90 ml (3 fl oz) boiling water

For the jam, heat the oil in a heavy pan and add the onions. Stir in a splash of water, reduce the heat to low and cover. Cook for 10 minutes, stirring occasionally, then add the garlic, chilli, cardamom and garam masala. Cook uncovered for 5 minutes more. Stir in the vinegar, scraping up any caramelised bits, then add the mango, golden syrup, salt and a splash of water. Reduce the heat to low, cover and cook for 10 minutes. Mash with a potato masher to break down the mango. Gently cook, uncovered, for 5 minutes until thick and jammy. Set aside to cool.

To make the pastries, toast the caraway seeds in a dry frying pan until fragrant. Set aside to cool.

In a medium bowl, whisk together the flour, salt and caraway seeds. Stir in the vegetable oil and the boiling water. Bring the dough together and knead until smooth. Cut into 30 equal pieces, then shape into balls. Roll out into 10 cm (4 inch) discs and prick all over with a fork.

Pour enough oil into a large pan to come 5 cm (2 inches) up the sides. Heat to 170°C (325°F) – the oil is hot enough when a small piece of bread turns golden in 30 seconds. Deep-fry the discs 2 or 3 at a time for about 1 minute, turning them over in the oil so they turn golden all over. Transfer to a wire rack lined with paper towels. Serve hot with a bowl of the jam alongside.

chickpea bites

WITH ROAST PEPPER TAPENADE

These tasty bites are perfect finger food to serve with drinks. Ras el hanout is widely available these days, but if you can't find this wonderful spice use ½ teaspoon ground cumin mixed with ½ teaspoon ground coriander instead.

MAKES: 20
PREPARATION: 20 minutes
COOKING: 15 minutes

120 g (4¼ oz) tinned chickpeas (drained weight), drained and rinsed
70 g (2½ oz) rice flour, plus more for sprinkling
½ teaspoon sea salt flakes
½ flax egg (*see* p 17)
1 teaspoon ras el hanout
1 tablespoon olive oil, plus extra for brushing
1 teaspoon nigella seeds (optional)

FOR THE TAPENADE
300 g (10½ oz) red capsicum (peppers) in oil (drained weight)
½ garlic clove
2 teaspoons capers, rinsed
3 tablespoons chopped coriander (cilantro), plus extra sprigs to serve
1 tablespoon extra virgin olive oil
freshly ground black pepper

Heat the oven to 180°C (350°F/Gas 4). Blitz the chickpeas in a food processor to a paste. Transfer to a mixing bowl and add the flour, salt, flax egg, ras el hanout and the olive oil. Mix well, then gradually add about 70 ml (2¼ fl oz) water – use just enough to form a dough that will roll out without crumbling. Knead for a minute or so. Shape into a disc, put between 2 sheets of baking paper and roll out to a thickness of 4 mm. Peel back the top layer of paper and stamp out 5 cm (2 inch) circles with a cookie cutter. Transfer to a baking tray lined with baking paper. Brush with olive oil and sprinkle with the nigella seeds (if using), gently pressing them into the dough.

Bake for about 15 minutes, or until firm and pale gold. Transfer to a wire rack to cool.

Meanwhile, to make the tapenade, put the peppers, garlic, capers, chopped coriander and the extra virgin olive oil in a food processor. Blitz to a rough sauce. Season with salt and pepper.

To serve, spoon 1 teaspoon of the tapenade onto each chickpea bite and top with a coriander sprig.

vegetable fritters

WITH DIPPING SAUCE

It's important to keep the ingredients chilled to produce batter that turns lovely and crisp when deep-fried. These fritters must be eaten as soon as they're cooked, which shouldn't be a problem.

SERVES: 4
PREPARATION: 15 minutes
COOKING: 15 minutes

400 g (14 oz) mixed vegetables, such as sweet potato, potato, zucchini (courgettes), carrots, eggplant (aubergines), mushrooms, broccoli, red capsicum (pepper) and cauliflower
about 1 litre (35 fl oz/4 cups) vegetable oil, for deep-frying
85 g (3 oz) plain (all-purpose) flour, sifted and chilled
1 tablespoon potato starch or cornflour (cornmeal)
½ teaspoon fine sea salt
200 ml (7 fl oz) ice-cold sparkling mineral water

FOR THE DIPPING SAUCE
90 ml (3 fl oz) rice vinegar
2 tablespoons caster (superfine) sugar
1 tablespoon soy sauce or tamari
1 teaspoon grated fresh ginger
1 squeeze lime juice
½ green chilli, finely sliced

Peel the vegetables if necessary. Cut the sweet potato, potato, zucchini, carrots and eggplant into 3 mm (⅛ inch) slices. Cut vegetables like mushrooms, cauliflower and broccoli into bite-sized chunks. Refrigerate while you prepare the rest of the dish.

Whisk together the dipping sauce ingredients.

Pour enough oil into a frying pan or shallow saucepan to come 5 cm (2 inches) up the sides. Heat to 170°C (325°F) – the oil is hot enough when a small piece of bread turns golden in 30 seconds.

While the oil is heating – not earlier – mix the flour, potato starch or cornflour, salt and mineral water together with a fork until just combined. Don't mix too much – lumps are fine. When the oil is hot enough, dip the vegetables into the batter one at a time, gently shaking off any excess, then carefully put in the hot oil.

Cook in small batches until golden, turning the vegetables to achieve an even colour. You might need to adjust the heat to prevent the oil from getting too hot. Transfer to paper towels with a slotted spoon. Serve immediately with the dipping sauce.

filled sweet potato skins

WITH CITRUS SOUR CREAM

The combination of sweet potato with a cheesy,
herby filling is pretty magical.

SERVES: 2–4
PREPARATION: 20 minutes
COOKING: 50 minutes

3 small sweet potatoes, about 750 g (1 lb 10 oz)
2 tablespoons vegan parmesan cheese,
home-made (*see* p 102) or grated shop-bought
1 generous pinch chilli flakes
1 heaped tablespoon finely
sliced spring onion (scallion)
150 ml (5 fl oz) non-dairy sour cream

finely grated zest of 1 lemon
1 tablespoon chopped fresh thyme
1 tablespoon chopped flat-leaf (Italian) parsley
sea salt flakes
freshly ground black pepper
4 tablespoons breadcrumbs
olive oil, for drizzling

Heat the oven to 200°C (400°F/Gas 6). Put the whole sweet potatoes on a baking tray and bake for about 40 minutes, or until very soft. While still hot, cut in half lengthways and carefully scoop most of the flesh into a bowl, leaving a layer of flesh on the skin. Be careful not to tear the skin. Add the parmesan cheese, chilli flakes, spring onion, 2 tablespoons of the sour cream, half the lemon zest and all the herbs to the sweet potato flesh. Mix well and season with salt and pepper.

Spoon the filling back into the sweet potato cases. Don't worry that the skins seem very soft as they will crisp up when returned to the oven. Sprinkle over the breadcrumbs and drizzle with olive oil. Bake for 10 minutes, or until the topping is golden and the filling warmed through. Meanwhile, mix the remaining sour cream with the remaining lemon zest.

Leave the sweet potato halves whole, or cut in half if you are serving these as finger food. Serve with the sour cream on the side.

zucchini & farro fritters

WITH LEMON & MINT

The farro makes these fritters quite filling and gives them a pleasing, slightly chewy texture. Cooking time for farro varies wildly and often the packet doesn't offer guidance. Here, the cooking time provided is for pearled farro (about 12 minutes) but you might need longer.

MAKES: 16 small or 8 large fritters
PREPARATION: 20 minutes
COOKING: 25 minutes (more for unpearled farro), plus 15 minutes cooling

75 g pearled farro
200 g (7 oz) grated zucchini (courgette)
finely grated zest of 1 lemon, plus 1 squeeze lemon juice
70 g (2½ oz) non-dairy mozzarella or other cheese, grated

3 tablespoons plain (all-purpose) flour
3–4 tablespoon olive oil
10 mint leaves, chopped
sea salt flakes
freshly ground black pepper

Cook the farro following the packet directions. Drain well, rinse in cold water and spread out on a large plate to cool and dry, about 15 minutes.

Meanwhile, wrap the grated zucchini in a clean tea towel (dish towel) and squeeze out as much liquid as possible. Put in a mixing bowl with the lemon zest, cheese, flour, 1 tablespoon of the olive oil, the mint and salt and pepper. Mix with your hands, squeezing to bring the ingredients together. Shape into patties about 1 cm (½ inch) thick – the size will depend on whether you want small or large fritters.

Heat 2 tablespoons of the remaining olive oil in a frying pan and fry the patties for 3–4 minutes on each side, until crisp and golden. Add more oil if necessary. Serve hot, with a squeeze of lemon juice over the top and extra salt to taste.

pumpkin & corn blinis

WITH SOUR CREAM

These are very tasty little canapés or starters. The suggested spoonfuls of batter make 5 cm (2 inch) blinis, but you can make them slightly smaller if you are serving them as finger food.

MAKES: about 15
PREPARATION: 10 minutes
COOKING: 25 minutes

175 g (6 oz) peeled and chopped pumpkin (squash)
125 g (4½ oz) self-raising flour
1 pinch fine sea salt
1 large pinch grated nutmeg
½ teaspoon baking powder
1 tablespoon vegetable oil, plus extra for frying
250 ml (9 fl oz/1 cup) non-dairy milk

40 g (1½ oz) sweetcorn kernels from a tin, plus 2 tablespoons extra to serve (optional)
sea salt flakes
freshly ground black pepper
230 ml (7¾ fl oz)non-dairy sour cream
1 tablespoon olive oil
1 tablespoon lemon juice

Steam the pumpkin until very tender and mash or blitz to a smooth purée. Set aside to cool.

Meanwhile, combine the flour, salt, nutmeg and baking powder in a mixing bowl. Make a well in the centre and slowly beat in the vegetable oil and then the milk. Whisk to beat out any lumps. Stir in the pumpkin until completely amalgamated and then add the sweetcorn. Season generously with salt and pepper. Set aside.

Whisk together the sour cream, olive oil, lemon juice and salt and pepper.

Heat a little vegetable oil in a heavy frying pan and wipe out any excess with paper towels. Drop in dessertspoonfuls of the batter and cook for a couple of minutes until golden underneath. Flip and fry for another 30 seconds or until cooked through. Transfer to a warm plate and cover loosely with foil.

Serve the blinis with a spoonful of the sour cream, corn kernels (if using) and some black pepper.

roasted seaweed snacks

Crisp and flavoursome, seaweed chips are a popular and healthy packaged snack, but they're very easy to make from scratch. You can play around with the seasonings: add more chilli powder, use paprika instead or leave out the sugar. Go easy with the salt as they don't need very much.

MAKES: about 32
PREPARATION: 10 minutes
COOKING: 25 minutes

60 ml (2 fl oz/¼ cup) vegetable oil
2 tablespoons sesame oil
½ teaspoon chilli powder

2 teaspoons soft light brown sugar
4 nori sheets
sea salt flakes, for sprinkling

Heat the oven to 170°C (325°F/Gas 3). Mix together the oils, chilli powder and sugar in a small bowl. Very lightly brush each nori sheet with the oil mixture right up to the edges. Cut each sheet into quarters and then cut each quarter in half to make 8 rectangles. Transfer to a baking tray and roast for about 25 minutes, or until starting to crisp up and pucker. They will crisp up further as they cool. Sprinkle with a touch of salt, as desired.

bahn mi

WITH CRISPY TOFU & PICKLED VEGETABLES

Pickled vegetables are wonderful accompaniments to food like burgers (*see* pp 96–7), so I recommend making double so you have some on hand for later. You can store them in the fridge, covered, for at least 4 weeks.

MAKES: 2 large baguettes
PREPARATION: 20 minutes, plus 1 hour 45 minutes cooling and marinating
COOKING: 10 minutes

FOR THE PICKLED VEGETABLES
2 cups julienned vegetables, such as carrots, cucumbers (seeds removed), daikon radishes or capsicums (peppers)
1 teaspoon fine sea salt
2 teaspoons plus 2 tablespoons caster (superfine) sugar
125 ml (4 fl oz/½ cup) white wine vinegar
1 tablespoon sea salt flakes
½ tablespoon coriander seeds, crushed
½ tablespoon mustard seeds, crushed

FOR THE REST OF THE DISH
400 g (14 oz) tofu, pressed and drained (*see* p 15)
2 tablespoons rapeseed or vegetable oil
2 x 10 cm (4 inch) lengths baguette
1 small handful coriander (cilantro), coarsely chopped
1 small handful mint, coarsely chopped

Start by making the pickled vegetables. Put the vegetables in a bowl and sprinkle with the fine sea salt and the 2 teaspoons sugar. Toss and massage the salt and sugar into the vegetables. Put in a colander set over a bowl and leave to drain.

Meanwhile, in a pan, combine the vinegar, the 2 tablespoons sugar, the sea salt flakes, coriander seeds and mustard seeds. Bring to the boil and stir to dissolve the salt and sugar. Remove from the heat, add 125 ml (4 fl oz/½ cup) cold water, pour into a bowl and set aside to cool, about 45 minutes.

Rinse the vegetables, put in a clean tea towel (dish towel) and squeeze out the liquid. Put in

an airtight container. Pour over the salt and sugar mixture. Leave to marinate for at least 1 hour before serving.

To make the bahn mi, cut the tofu into bite-sized pieces. Heat the oil in a frying pan and fry the tofu over a medium–high heat until crisp and golden on all sides. Drain on paper towels and set aside to keep warm.

Slice the baguette pieces in half, fill with the tofu, herbs and pickled vegetables and serve immediately.

mushroom & avocado panini

In our household, these fast and easy cooked sandwiches are fondly known as 'squishes'. Play around with the ingredients if you like by adding a little dairy-free sour cream, a pinch of chilli flakes or different fresh herbs.

SERVES: 1–2
PREPARATION: 5 minutes
COOKING: about 6 minutes

2 tablespoons olive oil, plus extra for brushing
200 g (7 oz) fresh mushrooms, sliced
1 garlic clove, finely chopped
2 tablespoons lemon juice, plus extra to taste
1 small handful flat-leaf (Italian) parsley, chopped

sea salt flakes
freshly ground black pepper
1 ripe avocado
1 large flour tortilla

Heat the olive oil in a large frying pan and add the mushrooms and garlic. Cook over a medium heat, stirring often, until the mushrooms are soft and juicy. Add 1 tablespoon of the lemon juice and all of the parsley and season well with salt and pepper. Cook for a couple more minutes, stirring. Reduce the heat to low and leave the pan slightly off the heat to keep warm.

Cut the avocado in half, remove the stone and scoop the flesh into a bowl. Mash well, add the remaining lemon juice and season with salt and pepper. Put the tortilla on a clean chopping board and spread the mashed avocado on the lower half. Top with the cooked mushrooms and then fold the top half over to make a semi-circle. Press down gently. Heat a griddle or frying pan over a medium–high heat, brush with oil and cook the filled tortilla for 3–4 minutes on each side, gently pressing down with a spatula, until golden or charred. Serve immediately.

SIX IDEAS
FOR

burgers

+++ +++

Serve these burgers inside buns with whatever salad, pickles or condiments you fancy. Onion relish, chutney and chilli sauce work well, or stir harissa paste, chipotle paste, lime zest or crushed garlic into non-dairy mayonnaise.

JUICY BLACK BEAN

Soak 10 g (¼ oz) dried porcini mushrooms in hot water. Drain and chop. Fry 1 chopped onion in olive oil. Add 2 sliced garlic cloves, the porcini, salt and pepper. Cook for 5 minutes. Add 1 tbsp balsamic vinegar. Stir until evaporated. Blitz 15 g (½ oz) oats in a food processor and put in a bowl. Drain and rinse 1 x 400 g (14 oz) tinned black beans. Blitz half and add to oats. Add unblitzed beans, 150 g (5½ oz) grated cooked beetroot (beets), liquid squeezed out, 100 g (3½ oz) cooked rice, the onion, 1 tsp chipotle paste, ½ tsp paprika, ground cumin and coriander, 1 tbsp tomato sauce (ketchup), grated zest of ½ lime, 1 tbsp chopped coriander (cilantro) and 15 g (½ oz) breadcrumbs. Shape into 4 patties and chill. Fry in olive oil until golden.

MUSHROOM

Remove the stalks from 4 portobello mushrooms. Whisk together 2 tbsp olive oil, 1 tsp chopped thyme and 2 crushed garlic cloves. Brush the open sides of the mushrooms with the oil and grill for 5 minutes. Turn over, brush with more of the oil and cook for 5 minutes more. Turn over again, brush with more oil, then sprinkle with 2 tsp vegan parmesan cheese, either home-made (*see* p 102) or grated shop-bought. Grill until bubbling.

LENTIL

Mix 250 g (9 oz) cold mashed potato with 200 g (7 oz) cooked green or brown lentils, 1 tsp garam masala, 2 tbsp breadcrumbs, 1 finely sliced spring onion (scallion) and sea salt flakes and freshly ground black pepper. Form into 4 patties and chill for 30 minutes. Fry in olive oil until golden.

KIBBE

Fry 1 chopped onion in olive oil until soft. Add 1 chopped garlic clove, 1/2 tsp each allspice, cinnamon and cumin and cook for 2 minutes. Add 90 g (3¼ oz) red lentils, 1/2 tsp fine sea salt and 800 ml (28 fl oz) water. Gently cook, covered, for 20 minutes. Add 90 g (3¼ oz) rinsed burghul (bulgur) wheat and cook for 20 minutes, or until tender. Drain, return to the pan and add 1/2 tbsp tomato paste (concentrated purée), 2 tbsp pine nuts and 1 tbsp pomegranate molasses. Cook for 2 minutes more then leave to cool. Add 1 small handful each chopped mint and flat-leaf (Italian) parsley and 1 tbsp rice flour. Shape into 4 patties and fry in vegetable oil until golden.

CHORIZO

Crumble 225 g (8 oz) tempeh into a bowl. In a separate bowl, whisk together 1 tbsp miso paste, 3 tbsp soy sauce, 2 tbsp tomato paste (concentrated purée), 1/2 tsp each smoked paprika and cayenne pepper, 1 tsp dried oregano and 2 tbsp vegetable stock. Pour over the tempeh and mix well. Shape into 4 patties and fry in olive oil until golden on both sides.

WHITE BEAN

Fry 1 finely chopped onion and 1/2 a finely chopped red capsicum (pepper) in olive oil until soft. Add 1 crushed garlic clove, 1/2 tsp each ground cumin and coriander and a pinch of chilli powder. Cook for 2 minutes, then set aside to cool. Drain 1 x 400 g (14 oz) tinned cannellini beans and blitz two-thirds in a blender with 2 tbsp extra virgin olive oil and salt and pepper. Stir together the blitzed and unblitzed beans, 2 tbsp breadcrumbs, 2 tsp chipotle paste and the onion mixture. Taste for seasoning. Shape into 4 patties and chill for 30 minutes. Fry in olive oil over a medium heat until golden.

CHAPTER 4

soups & cold salads

+++

onion soup

WITH CHEESY TOAST

Gosh this is good. The trick is to cook the onions long and slow so their flavour really mellows and sweetens. You can use simple vegetable stock but the 'meaty' quality of porcini mushrooms adds depth of flavour.

SERVES: 4
PREPARATION: 30 minutes
COOKING: about 1 hour

40 g (1½ oz) dried porcini mushrooms
250 ml (9 fl oz/1 cup) boiling water
3 tablespoons olive oil
750 g (1 lb 10 oz) onions, finely sliced
1 teaspoon soft light brown sugar
2 tablespoons dry sherry
600 ml (21 fl oz) porcini mushroom stock

sea salt flakes
freshly ground black pepper
4 slices country-style bread
4 heaped tablespoons grated non-dairy cheese, plus extra to serve
1 squeeze lemon juice

In a small bowl, cover the porcini mushrooms with the boiling water. Set aside to soak for 30 minutes. Drain, squeeze out excess liquid and reserve the soaking liquor.

Meanwhile, in a heavy pan, heat the oil over a medium heat and add the onions. Stir to coat in the oil and add a splash of water. Reduce the heat to low, cover and gently cook for about 45 minutes. Take the lid off and stir occasionally during this time to ensure the onions are not sticking to the pan, adding a splash more water if needed. Increase the heat, stir in the sugar and cook for a few more minutes uncovered until starting to caramelise. Add the sherry,

stock and reserved porcini soaking liquor and bring to the boil. Reduce the heat, season with salt and pepper and gently simmer for 10 minutes.

While the soup is simmering, toast the bread, top with the cheese and put under a hot grill (broiler) until the cheese is bubbling and melted. Add the squeeze of lemon juice to the soup and taste for seasoning. Put the cheesy toast in the bowls and ladle over the soup. Alternatively, serve the toast alongside.

SIX IDEAS FOR

cheese

+++ +++

These are very tasty cheese substitutes. Play around with flavourings and add things like chopped fresh herbs, cracked black peppercorns instead of white pepper, chilli flakes or garlic powder.

CHEDDAR

Soak 40 g (1½ oz/¼ cup) raw cashew nuts in water for at least 4 hours. Drain and rinse. Blitz in a food processor with 3 tbsp nutritional yeast, ½ tsp celery salt, ½ tsp sea salt flakes and a pinch each of white pepper and mustard powder. In a pan, whisk 200 ml (7 fl oz) unsweetened soya milk with 4 tsp agar-agar powder and 1 tbsp olive oil. Cook for 5 minutes until thick, then add to the nut mixture with 4 tbsp lemon juice. Blitz. Pour into an oiled ramekin, smooth the top and cover. Chill until set, then invert onto a plate.

Makes about 185 g (6½ oz)

RICOTTA

In a food processor, put 250 g (9 oz) firm tofu (drained and dried with paper towels), 2 tsp lemon juice, 2 tsp olive oil, ½ minced garlic clove, ½ tsp sea salt flakes and freshly ground black pepper. Pulse until combined. Don't over-process or the tofu will turn to a paste – you want to retain a bit of texture.

Makes about 250 g (9 oz)

PARMESAN

Lightly toast 70 g (2½ oz) sesame seeds in a dry frying pan until fragrant and pale gold. Be careful not to burn. Transfer to a blender or food processor and add 3 tbsp nutritional yeast, a pinch of fine sea salt and a pinch of white pepper. Pulse until well combined. Store in an airtight container.

Makes about 120 g (4¼ oz)

 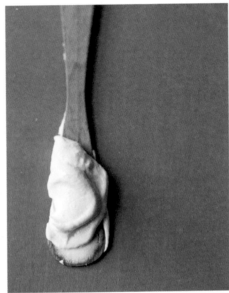 

GOAT'S CHEESE

Soak 160 g raw cashew nuts in water for at least 4 hours. Drain and rinse well. Put in a blender with 2 tbsp water, 4 g probiotic powder, a pinch of fine sea salt and 2 tbsp water. Blitz to a smooth paste. Scrape into a bowl, cover with plastic wrap and set aside somewhere warm for 12 hours. Stir in 2 tbsp white wine vinegar and 2 tsp nutritional yeast. Set aside in the fridge for 24–48 hours until firm.

Makes about 200 g (7 oz)

CREAM CHEESE

Soak 40 g (1½ oz/¼ cup) raw cashew nuts for at least 4 hours. Drain, rinse well and blitz together with 300 g (10½ oz) silken tofu, 2 tsp agave nectar, 2 tsp lemon juice, 1 tsp xanthan gum and ½ tsp fine sea salt and a pinch of white pepper. Chill.

Makes about 350 g (12 oz)

CHEESE SAUCE

In a small pan, combine 200 ml (7 fl oz) vegetable stock and 1½ tsp white miso paste. Whisk over a medium heat until combined. Reduce the heat, add 1 tsp each of garlic and onion granules, 125 ml (4 fl oz/½ cup) cashew cream (*see* p 26) and season with salt and pepper. Stir continuously for about 5 minutes until the mixture has thickened into a creamy sauce. Remove from the heat and stir in 60 g (2¼ oz) grated non-dairy cheese until melted.

Makes about 200 ml (7 fl oz)

corn chowder

Rich and hearty, this is a delicious and satisfying soup. I generally use rice milk as its mild flavour doesn't detract from the sweetness of the corn, but any non-dairy milk will work well.

SERVES: 4–6
PREPARATION: 15 minutes
COOKING: about 30 minutes

2 tablespoons olive oil
1 celery stalk, finely chopped
1 white onion, finely chopped
sea salt flakes
freshly ground black pepper
2 garlic cloves, finely sliced
300 g (10½ oz) peeled and diced potatoes
3 tablespoons plain (all-purpose) flour

750 ml (26 fl oz/3 cups) hot vegetable stock, plus 250 ml (9 fl oz/1 cup) extra for thinning if needed
400 ml (14 fl oz) unsweetened rice milk
4 corn cobs, kernels sliced off with a sharp knife
3 tablespoons chopped tarragon, plus extra leaves to serve
1 squeeze lemon juice

Heat the olive oil in a heavy pan, add the celery and onion and season with salt and pepper. Fry over a medium heat until tender. Add the garlic and cook for a few minutes more. Stir in the potatoes, sprinkle with the flour and cook over a medium heat for a couple of minutes, stirring constantly. Add the 750 ml (26 fl oz/3 cups) hot stock, the milk, most of the corn (reserving some to serve) and the chopped tarragon. Simmer for 10–15 minutes until the corn and potatoes are tender.

Set aside to cool a little, then carefully transfer to a blender. You will probably need to blitz the chowder in 2 batches or more. If your blender is not powerful enough, pass the chowder through a sieve to make it completely smooth. Return the blitzed or strained chowder to a clean pan and add extra stock or water to achieve the consistency you like. Add the squeeze of lemon juice and taste for seasoning. Stir over a medium heat to warm through.

Ladle into bowls and sprinkle over the remaining corn kernels and the tarragon leaves. Delicious served with crusty bread.

soup au pistou

This flavoursome soup belies the simplicity of its ingredients. The amount of pistou might look meagre but it's so intensely flavoured you only need a heaped teaspoonful or so for each serving.

SERVES: 6–8
PREPARATION: 20 minutes
COOKING: 25 minutes

FOR THE SOUP
3 tablespoons olive oil
3 medium carrots, peeled and chopped into rounds
2 medium potatoes, peeled and chopped into 2 cm (¾ inch) dice
2 celery stalks, finely chopped
1 onion, finely chopped
2 garlic cloves, finely chopped
½ medium zucchini (courgette), cut in half lengthways and sliced into half-moons
120 g (4¼ oz) savoy cabbage, shredded

2 litres (7 fl oz/8 cups) vegetable stock or water
2 thyme sprigs
2 x 3 cm (1¼ inch) strips lemon zest
sea salt flakes
freshly ground black pepper

FOR THE PISTOU
75 g basil leaves
3 tablespoons extra virgin olive oil
½ teaspoon sea salt flakes, or more to taste
2 garlic cloves, chopped

Heat the oil in a large, heavy lidded pan and add the carrots, potatoes, celery and onion. Cook gently for about 12 minutes, stirring and turning the vegetables over every now and then. Add a splash of water if the vegetables start to stick to the pan. Add the garlic, zucchini and cabbage and cook for a few minutes more. Add the stock or water, thyme and lemon zest. Season with salt and pepper and gently simmer, covered, for about 10 minutes.

To make the pistou, blitz all the ingredients in a mini food processor, or pound in a mortar. Taste for seasoning.

To serve, ladle the soup into bowls and top with a spoonful of the pistou. Wonderful served with warm country-style bread.

roast garlic soup

WITH CRISPY CHICKPEA CROUTONS

Yes, there is a lot of garlic in this soup but the
roasting mellows its flavour.

SERVES: 2 generously
PREPARATION: 15 minutes
COOKING: 40 minutes

4 large garlic bulbs, cut in half
230 ml (7¾ fl oz) olive oil
3 tablespoons plain (all-purpose) flour
1 litre (35 fl oz/4 cups) vegetable stock
120 g (4¼ oz) tinned chickpeas
(drained weight)

½ teaspoon cayenne pepper
½ teaspoon smoked paprika
sea salt flakes
freshly ground black pepper
1 squeeze lime juice

Heat the oven to 170°C (325°F/Gas 3). Put the garlic cut-side down in an ovenproof pan. Add 200 ml (7 fl oz) of the olive oil and transfer to the oven. After 20 minutes, check the underside of the garlic – the cloves should be golden and starting to caramelise. If the cloves are turning brown too quickly, turn them over and continue cooking until the cloves are very soft. When cooked, lift out with a slotted spoon and carefully remove the cloves from their skins using the point of a knife or a fork.

Remove and discard 90 ml (3 fl oz) of the oil from the pan, put the garlic cloves back in and sprinkle over the flour. Stir over a medium heat, mashing the garlic if necessary with the back of a spoon, until the mixture is smooth. Add the stock, stir, then very gently simmer for 10–15 minutes.

Meanwhile, dry the chickpeas with paper towels and briskly rub in a tea towel (dish towel) to remove as much skin as possible. Combine the cayenne pepper and paprika in a small bowl. Heat the remaining olive oil in a frying pan, add the chickpeas and fry for 10 minutes, or until crisp and golden. Drain in a sieve, transfer to a bowl and then toss with the spices.

Blitz the soup in a blender until creamy. Return to the pan, add the squeeze of lime juice and taste for seasoning. Serve sprinkled with the spiced chickpeas.

sweet potato soup

WITH PUMPERNICKEL CROUTONS

Sweet potato and curry are excellent partners, and this soup
sings with flavour without tasting strongly of curry.

SERVES: 4
PREPARATION: 15 minutes
COOKING: 40 minutes

4 tablespoons olive oil
1 onion, chopped
2 garlic cloves, finely chopped
1 teaspoon mild curry powder
750 g (l lb 10 oz/5⅓ cups) sweet potato,
peeled and chopped
1 apple, peeled, cored and chopped

1.25 litres (44 fl oz/5 cups) vegetable stock
60 ml (2 fl oz/¼ cup) coconut milk
juice of ½ lime
sea salt flakes
freshly ground black pepper
2 slices pumpernickel, cut into short strips

Heat 2 tablespoons of the olive oil in a heavy
pan and add the onion. Cook, stirring, over a
medium heat for 5 minutes until soft. Add the
garlic and curry powder and cook, stirring, for
a few minutes more. Add the sweet potato and
apple and stir well to combine with the other
ingredients. Cook, stirring frequently, until the
sweet potato starts to brown at the edges,
about 15 minutes. Keep adjusting the heat to
prevent the onion burning.

Pour in 1 litre (35 fl oz/4 cups) of the stock and
stir, scraping up the caramelised bits from the
bottom of the pan. Gently simmer, uncovered,
for 20 minutes, or until the sweet potato is
tender. Carefully transfer to a blender and blitz

until smooth. Pour into a clean pan and add
more of the remaining stock if the soup is too
thick for your liking. Add the coconut milk and
lime juice and season with salt and pepper.
The soup might need lots of salt, depending
on the saltiness of the stock. Keep warm while
you make the croutons.

Heat the remaining olive oil in a frying pan
and add the pumpernickel. Cook over a
medium–high heat, shaking the pan, until
the bread starts to crisp up. Remove to paper
towels to soak up excess oil.

Serve the soup immediately, sprinkled
with croutons.

matchstick salad

WITH AGAVE MUSTARD DRESSING

This is a beautiful salad, a little like slaw but lighter and fresher, with a citrusy agave dressing instead of a creamy one. Try to get the matchsticks as thin as possible but avoid using a box grater or you will end up with salad mush.

SERVES: 4 generously as a side
PREPARATION: 15 minutes, plus 15 minutes soaking
COOKING: none

3 medium carrots, peeled and
cut into matchsticks
30 g (1 oz) sultanas (golden raisins)
60 ml (2 fl oz/¼ cup) orange juice
1 handful pistachio nuts, toasted in a dry pan
1 medium raw beetroot (beet), peeled and
cut into matchsticks
½ red capsicum (pepper), cut into matchsticks
1 tablespoon chopped thyme
3 tablespoons chopped flat-leaf (Italian) parsley

FOR THE DRESSING
1½ tablespoons lemon juice
40 ml (1¼ fl oz) extra virgin olive oil
½ tablespoon agave nectar
½ teaspoon dijon mustard
sea salt flakes
freshly ground black pepper

Combine the carrots, sultanas and orange juice in a bowl and leave to soak for 15 minutes. Drain well, discard the juice and squeeze out excess liquid. Meanwhile, whisk together the dressing ingredients.

In a shallow serving bowl, combine the carrots, sultanas, pistachio nuts, beetroot, capsicum and herbs. Gently toss with just enough of the dressing to coat. Serve immediately.

sprouted salad

WITH MINTY SEED DRESSING

This is a very wholesome salad that's bursting with fresh flavours. There's plenty of room to tweak the ingredients according to what you have on hand. Use barley, wild rice or other grains instead of farro or brown rice, or use your favourite nuts or seeds.

SERVES: 2–4
PREPARATION: 10 minutes
COOKING: about 10–15 minutes

70 g (2½ oz/⅓ cup) farro or brown rice
150 g (5½ oz) mixed sprouts
1 carrot, grated
1 avocado

FOR THE DRESSING
3 tablespoons chopped mint
2 tablespoons extra virgin olive oil
2 tablespoons vegetable oil
2 tablespoons lemon juice
1 garlic clove, finely chopped
1 tablespoon sunflower seeds
sea salt flakes
freshly ground black pepper

Cook the farro or rice following the packet directions, being careful not to overcook. Drain, rinse in cold water and spread out on a large plate to cool. Pat dry with paper towels.

Meanwhile, whisk together the dressing ingredients, using 2 tablespoons of the mint.

When the grains are cool, put in a salad bowl and add the sprouts and carrot. Pour over the dressing and toss to combine – clean hands work best here. Halve the avocado, remove the stone and peel. Cut into slices or chunks and gently toss through the salad. Scatter with the remaining mint and serve immediately.

radish ceviche

This is a wonderfully vibrant-tasting salad, and very pretty too. It is best to use a mandoline here – a very handy piece of kitchen equipment – but if you don't have one just slice the vegetables as thinly (and carefully!) as you can.

SERVES: 2–4
PREPARATION: 10 minutes
COOKING: none

1 tablespoon lime juice
3 tablespoons olive oil
sea salt flakes
freshly ground black pepper
100 g (3½ oz) radishes, the largest available

70 g (2½ oz) cucumber, whole
½ red onion, peeled
2 tablespoons chopped mint, to serve
dill fronds, to serve

Whisk together the lime juice and olive oil. Season with salt and pepper and set aside.

Thinly slice the radishes, cucumber and onion, ideally on a mandoline: you will end up with discs of radish and cucumber and half-moons of onion.

Put the vegetables in a shallow bowl and toss with the dressing. Cover with plastic wrap and set aside for 20 minutes.

Serve sprinkled with mint and the dill fronds.

watermelon & coriander salad

Make sure the watermelon is chilled for this recipe so that the salad is crisp and refreshing. It makes a lovely starter on a summer's day.

SERVES: 4 as a side or starter
PREPARATION: 10 minutes
COOKING: 2 minutes

1 red onion, very finely sliced, ideally on a mandoline
3 tablespoons lime juice, plus extra to taste
1 tablespoon coriander seeds
1/2 teaspoon sea salt flakes
freshly ground black pepper

1/4 teaspoon cayenne pepper
1/2 teaspoon ground cumin
500 g (1 lb 2 oz) watermelon, cut into bite-sized pieces
200 g (7 oz) peeled and diced cucumber
3 tablespoons chopped coriander (cilantro)

Put the onion in a small bowl and pour over the lime juice. Set aside.

Toast the coriander seeds in a dry frying pan until fragrant. Transfer to a mortar and lightly crush. Mix with the salt, black pepper, cayenne pepper and cumin.

Gently combine the watermelon, cucumber, marinated onion and chopped coriander in a large bowl. Sprinkle over the spice mix and toss. Taste for seasoning and add more lime juice, if you like.

lentil & cranberry salad

Puy lentils look and taste wonderful with the red cranberries and green rocket. If you want to eat this salad warm, don't spread the lentils out to cool, just toss with the dressing while hot.

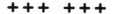

SERVES: 4
PREPARATION: 10 minutes
COOKING: about 35 minutes, plus 30 minutes cooling

1 clove
1 onion, peeled
2 bay leaves
800 ml (28 fl oz) vegetable stock
250 g (9 oz) puy lentils or tiny blue-green lentils, rinsed
100 g (3½ oz) dried cranberries
1 large handful rocket (arugula) leaves

FOR THE DRESSING
2 tablespoons balsamic vinegar
100 ml (3½ fl oz) extra virgin olive oil
1 garlic clove, crushed
sea salt flakes
freshly ground black pepper
1 teaspoon dijon mustard

Stick the clove in the onion and put in a pan with the bay leaves, stock and lentils. Bring to the boil, reduce the heat and gently simmer for 30 minutes, or until the lentils are tender. Skim off any scum that rises to the top. Top up with water if needed to ensure the lentils are covered. Drain, discard the bay leaves and onion and spread out on a plate to cool.

Meanwhile, cover the cranberries in boiling water and set aside to plump up for 10 minutes. Whisk together the dressing ingredients.

Drain the cranberries and pat dry with paper towels. In a serving bowl, combine the cranberries, lentils and rocket and toss with enough of the dressing to coat well. Taste for seasoning: lentils often need quite a lot of salt. Serve immediately.

orange-scented quinoa salad

WITH PISTACHIO NUTS & DATES

This is a lovely fragrant salad that makes a wonderful
addition to a help-yourself spread.

SERVES: 4
PREPARATION: 20 minutes
COOKING: 18 minutes, plus 15 minutes cooling

175 g (6 oz) quinoa, rinsed
30 g (1 oz) shelled pistachio nuts
70 ml (2¼ fl oz) orange juice, plus the finely
grated zest of 1 orange
60 ml (2 fl oz/¼ cup) mild extra virgin olive oil
2 teaspoons sherry vinegar
sea salt flakes

freshly ground black pepper
6 spring onions (scallions), very finely sliced
3 tablespoons chopped mint
3 tablespoons chopped flat-leaf (Italian) parsley
1 large bunch watercress,
tough stalks removed
10 ready-to-eat dates, chopped

In a medium pan, bring 500 ml (17 fl oz/2 cups)
water to the boil. Add the quinoa, reduce the
heat to low, cover and cook for 18 minutes, or
until the water is absorbed. Remove from the
heat, fluff with a fork and spread out on a large
plate to cool.

In a dry frying pan, toast the pistachio nuts
until fragrant and starting to brown. Set aside
to cool, then coarsely chop.

To make the dressing, whisk together the
orange juice, olive oil, vinegar and salt
and pepper.

To assemble the salad, put the quinoa in a
large serving bowl and toss with half the
dressing. Fork through the orange zest, spring
onions, herbs, watercress, dates and enough
of the remaining dressing to coat. Taste for
seasoning and add more salt, pepper or
dressing if needed. Serve immediately.

Thai salad

Many Southeast Asian-style salads feature fish sauce in the dressing. Although vegan fish sauce is available – feel free to add some to the dressing if you like – this salad has bags of flavour without it. The noodles make this quite a substantial salad, so it's perfect as a main course.

SERVES: 2
PREPARATION: 20 minutes
COOKING: depends on type of noodles

FOR THE SALAD
100 g (3½ oz) rice noodles
a few drops sesame oil
90 g (3¼ oz) bean sprouts
½ red capsicum (pepper), seeded and finely sliced
50 g (1¾ oz) baby English spinach, sliced
1 red chilli, seeded and finely sliced
3 spring onions (scallions), finely sliced
¼ cucumber, peeled, halved and quartered lengthways, then finely sliced
¼ savoy cabbage, finely sliced

1 handful mint leaves, chopped
1 handful basil leaves, torn
1 handful coriander (cilantro) leaves, chopped
60 g (2¼ oz) peanuts, toasted and chopped

FOR THE DRESSING
90 ml (3 fl oz) lime juice
2 tablespoons soft brown sugar
1 teaspoon grated fresh ginger
2 garlic cloves, crushed
2 teaspoons sesame oil

Cook the noodles following the packet directions, rinse with cold water and toss with the sesame oil to avoid sticking. Set aside.

Whisk together the dressing ingredients.

Combine all the salad ingredients in a bowl, reserving some of the peanuts, coriander and chilli. Toss with enough of the dressing to coat. Serve immediately, sprinkled with the remaining peanuts, coriander and chilli.

herb & cabbage salad

WITH BURNT LEMON DRESSING

The burnt lemon dressing is a tangy counterpoint to the sweet dried fruit in this crunchy, tasty salad. Play around with the proportions of lemon juice and maple syrup to get the dressing just the way you like it.

SERVES: 2–4
PREPARATION: 10 minutes
COOKING: 5 minutes

150 g (5½ oz/1½ cups) snow peas (mangetout)
fine sea salt
½ lemon
3 tablespoons extra virgin olive oil
½ tablespoon maple syrup
sea salt flakes
freshly ground black pepper

150 g (5½ oz/2 cups) red cabbage, finely shredded
4 tablespoons chopped flat-leaf (Italian) parsley
4 tablespoons chopped coriander (cilantro)
3 tablespoons sunflower seeds
3 tablespoons goji berries

Blanch the snow peas in boiling salted water for 1 minute. Drain, refresh in cold water and drain again. Cut in half on the diagonal and set aside to dry.

Heat a frying pan or griddle pan until hot and cook the half lemon cut-side down for 3–5 minutes until charred. Squeeze out the juice and transfer 2 tablespoons to a bowl. Add the olive oil and maple syrup and whisk. Season with salt and pepper.

Combine the snow peas and remaining salad ingredients in a salad bowl. Toss with the dressing and serve immediately.

peach, bean & almond salad

You could make this salad with uncooked peaches but frying really coaxes out their delicious juices.

SERVES: 2–4
PREPARATION: 10 minutes
COOKING: 30 minutes

140 g (5 oz) buckwheat, rinsed
4 tablespoons olive oil
1 onion, thinly sliced
1 tablespoon chopped oregano
400 g (14 oz) firm ripe peaches, halved, stones removed and sliced
200 g (7 oz) green beans, blanched and refreshed in cold water
60 g (2¼ oz) toasted sliced almonds

FOR THE DRESSING
1½ tablespoons balsamic vinegar
75 ml extra virgin olive oil
1½ tablespoons agave nectar
sea salt flakes
freshly ground black pepper

Put the buckwheat in a dry lidded pan and toast over a medium heat until aromatic. Add 350 ml (12 fl oz) water, bring to the boil and reduce the heat to low. Cover and simmer for about 18 minutes – the buckwheat should be tender and the water absorbed. Fluff with a fork and spread out on a large plate to cool and dry out.

Meanwhile, heat 2 tablespoons of the olive oil in a frying pan and cook the onion for 5 minutes. Add the oregano and fry for

2 minutes more. Transfer the onion to a small bowl, wipe the pan clean and add the remaining olive oil. Cook the peaches until soft and starting to colour on both sides.

Whisk together the dressing ingredients.

Combine the buckwheat, onion and beans and toss with half of the dressing. Carefully fold through the peaches, almonds and enough of the remaining dressing to coat. Taste for seasoning and serve immediately.

tomato & cucumber panzanella salad

If you have stale bread to use up, this classic Italian salad is ideal.
As ever for simple dishes, good-quality ingredients are crucial, so use
lovely ripe tomatoes, flavourful olive oil and excellent bread.

SERVES: 2–4
PREPARATION: 15 minutes
COOKING: 5 minutes

2 garlic cloves
1½ tablespoons olive oil
120 g (4¼ oz) baguette, cut into cubes
400 g (14 oz) ripe tomatoes and
cherry tomatoes, mixed
45 ml (1½ fl oz) extra virgin olive oil

1 tablespoon white wine vinegar
sea salt flakes
freshly ground black pepper
1 large cucumber, peeled, halved lengthways
and cut into 5 mm (¼ inch) half moons
1 small handful basil leaves

Slice 1 of the garlic cloves. Pour the olive oil
into a cold frying pan and add the sliced garlic.
Gently cook until the oil heats and the garlic
starts to colour. Remove the garlic with a
slotted spoon and discard. Add the bread
to the oil, increase the heat to medium–high
and toss until crisp and golden. Transfer to
paper towels.

Cut the tomatoes into bite-sized pieces, put
in a colander set over a bowl and press down
lightly with the back of a spoon to release the
juices. Set aside.

Finely grate the remaining garlic clove into a
bowl. Add the extra virgin olive oil, the vinegar
and the tomato juices caught in the bowl
under the colander. Season generously with
salt and pepper and whisk.

Put the toasted bread, tomatoes, cucumber
and basil in a bowl. Add the dressing and
gently toss with your hands. The salad will
be fine to stand for up to 20 minutes before
serving to allow the flavours to mingle.

CHAPTER 5

warm salads & sides

+ + +

warm root vegetable & grain salad

WITH MAPLE SYRUP & CUMIN DRESSING

The root vegetables in this dish make it very filling and perfect for a main meal.
Change the vegetables if you like – potatoes, celeriac and chunks of capsicum
(peppers) also work well – but make sure you cut them into equal-sized pieces.

SERVES: 4
PREPARATION: 15 minutes
COOKING: 1 hour 5 minutes

2 parsnips, peeled and sliced in
half lengthways
4 medium carrots, about 500 g
(1 lb 2 oz), peeled
3 thyme sprigs
3 rosemary sprigs
4 tablespoons olive oil
sea salt flakes
freshly ground black pepper
2 red onions, halved
2 sweet potatoes, about 350 g (12 oz), peeled
and sliced lengthways into wedges
20 cherry tomatoes, about 250 g (9 oz/2 cups)

200 g (7 oz) mixed grains, such as farro,
freekeh, pearled barley and quinoa

FOR THE DRESSING
2 tablespoons maple syrup
2 tablespoons cider vinegar
125 ml (4 fl oz/½ cup) extra virgin olive oil
2 garlic cloves, crushed
¼ teaspoon ground cumin
sea salt flakes
freshly ground black pepper

Heat the oven to 190°C (375°F/Gas 5). In a large
baking tray, toss the parsnips, carrots, thyme and
rosemary with half of the olive oil. Season with
salt and pepper and roast for 20 minutes. Remove
the tray from the oven and add the onions, sweet
potatoes and the remaining olive oil. Season with
more salt and pepper and roast for a further
30 minutes. Add the tomatoes and cook for
15 minutes more.

Meanwhile, whisk together the dressing
ingredients. Taste for seasoning and add more
salt, pepper or vinegar if needed.

Cook the grains following the packet directions
until just tender. Be careful not to overcook. Drain,
add half of the dressing while the grains are still
hot and taste for seasoning. Keep warm until the
vegetables are ready.

When the vegetables are done, pour over most of
the remaining dressing and turn to coat. Gently
combine the grains and vegetables on a serving
plate and serve immediately, with the remaining
dressing poured over.

warm kale, barley & dried cherry salad

The earthy flavours in this substantial salad are wonderful.
As ever, be careful not to overcook the barley.

SERVES: 4 as a side
PREPARATION: 10 minutes, plus 15 minutes soaking
COOKING: about 30 minutes, depending on the barley

250 g (9 oz/1¼ cups) pearled barley
80 g (2¾ oz) dried cherries
2 tablespoons olive oil
150 g (5½ oz) trimmed (tough stalks removed) kale, shredded
1 small bunch flat-leaf (Italian) parsley, chopped

FOR THE DRESSING
4 tablespoons lemon juice
2 teaspoons dijon mustard
3 tablespoons extra virgin olive oil
sea salt flakes
freshly ground black pepper

Cook the barley following the packet directions until just tender and retaining some bite. Drain, rinse in cold water and spread out on a large plate. Pat dry with paper towels and set aside to cool. Meanwhile, cover the cherries with boiling water and leave to soften for 15 minutes, then drain. Whisk together the dressing ingredients.

Heat the 2 tablespoons olive oil in a frying pan and stir-fry the kale until tender but not completely wilted, about 4 minutes. Add the grains and cherries and cook, stirring, until just warmed through. Remove from the heat and stir through the parsley and the dressing. Taste for seasoning and add more salt and pepper if necessary. Serve warm.

roast beetroot & goat's cheese salad

If you feel like taking a shortcut here by using ready-cooked beetroot feel free, but roasting it yourself produces lots more flavour and is worth the time and effort.

SERVES: 4
PREPARATION: 15 minutes
COOKING: 1 hour 30 minutes

4 medium beetroot (beets), about 450 g (1 lb), scrubbed and trimmed
75 ml olive oil
sea salt flakes
freshly ground black pepper
1 thyme sprig, plus extra leaves for sprinkling

1 tablespoon balsamic vinegar
½ garlic clove, finely chopped
½ teaspoon dijon mustard
1 bunch watercress, thick stalks removed
60 g (2¼ oz) walnuts, lightly toasted
165 g (5¾ oz) non-dairy goat's cheese

Heat the oven to 180°C (350°F/Gas 4). Put the beetroots on a large piece of foil, drizzle with 2 tablespoons of the olive oil and season with salt and pepper. Add the thyme and close the foil parcel, sealing tightly. Put on a baking tray and roast for 1–1½ hours until very tender. When the beetroots are cool enough to handle, rub off the skins and cut into large bite-sized pieces. You can make the salad with warm beetroot or leave to cool to room temperature. Reserve the beetroot juices collected in the foil.

Meanwhile, whisk together the remaining olive oil, the vinegar, garlic, mustard and the reserved beetroot roasting juices when ready. Season with salt and pepper.

On a serving plate or shallow dish, combine the beetroot, watercress and walnuts and toss with the dressing. Top with spoonfuls of the goat's cheese and sprinkle over the thyme leaves. Serve immediately.

asparagus & mushrooms

WITH CHEESE SAUCE

Fresh morels instead of dried would also work brilliantly in this dish if you're lucky enough to be able to lay your hands on some. Just omit the soaking step if you do.

SERVES: 4
PREPARATION: 15 minutes, plus 30 minutes soaking
COOKING: about 10 minutes, once the cheese sauce is made

20 g (¾ oz) dried morel mushrooms
500 g (1 lb 2 oz) asparagus spears, tough ends removed
fine sea salt

3 tablespoons olive oil
165 g (5¾ oz) button mushrooms, thinly sliced
1 generous splash dry sherry
1 quantity cheese sauce (*see* p 103)

Put the morels in a bowl, cover with 300 ml (10½ fl oz) boiling water and set aside to soak for 30 minutes. Meanwhile, blanch the asparagus in boiling salted water for 1–2 minutes until almost cooked. Plunge into iced water to refresh, then drain. Set aside.

Drain the morels, reserving the soaking liquid, and rinse under cold running water. Squeeze out excess liquid, then coarsely chop and set aside.

In a small pan, heat 2 tablespoons of the olive oil and sauté the morels and button mushrooms for 5 minutes. Add the splash of sherry and let it bubble up. Reduce the heat, add the cheese sauce and enough of the reserved morel soaking liquid to make a thin but creamy sauce. Simmer for a minute or so, stirring. Set aside.

Heat the remaining olive oil in a frying pan and quickly stir-fry the asparagus to warm through. Tip out onto a serving plate, then spoon over the cheesy morel sauce. Serve immediately.

roast vegetable salad

WITH DUKKAH

Dukkah is a fragrant and spicy Middle Eastern condiment traditionally eaten with bread and good olive oil. This makes more dukkah than you need for the salad but it stores well in an airtight container for a couple of weeks.

SERVES: 4
PREPARATION: 30 minutes
COOKING: 45 minutes

FOR THE DUKKAH
30 g (1 oz) almonds or hazelnuts
30 g (1 oz) shelled pistachio nuts
4 tablespoons sesame seeds
2 tablespoons coriander seeds
2 tablespoons cumin seeds
1 teaspoon fennel seeds
1 teaspoon black peppercorns
2 teaspoons dried thyme
1 teaspoon sweet paprika
1 teaspoon fine sea salt

FOR THE SALAD
500 g (1 lb 2 oz) new potatoes, halved
500 g (1 lb 2 oz) sweet potato, peeled, cut into 4 cm (1½ inch) pieces
4 garlic cloves

2 tablespoons olive oil
sea salt flakes
freshly ground black pepper
1 large red capsicum (pepper), seeded and thickly sliced
1 large red onion, peeled and cut into wedges
80 g (2¾ oz) mix of rocket (arugula) and baby English spinach

FOR THE DRESSING
2 tablespoons lemon juice
60 ml (2 fl oz/¼ cup) extra virgin olive oil
2 teaspoons dijon mustard
2 tablespoons chopped oregano leaves
sea salt flakes
freshly ground black pepper

To make the dukkah, toast the nuts in a dry frying pan. Tip into a food processor and return the pan to the heat. Add the remaining dukkah ingredients to the pan except the thyme, paprika and salt. Toast as for the nuts, then transfer to the food processor. Add the thyme, paprika and salt and blitz. Don't overwork or the mixture will turn to a paste. Set aside.

Heat the oven to 220°C (425°F/Gas 7). In a baking tray, toss the potatoes, sweet potato and garlic with the olive oil. Season with salt and pepper and

roast for 20 minutes. Add the capsicum and onion, shake to coat in the oil and return to the oven for 10 minutes, or until the vegetables are tender and charred at the edges. Transfer to a plate to cool. Meanwhile, whisk together the dressing ingredients.

On a serving plate, combine the vegetables, rocket and spinach. Toss with enough dressing to coat. Sprinkle with some of the dukkah and serve while the vegetables are warm. Serve more dukkah alongside.

saffron roasted tomatoes

WITH HERBED TOFU

Tomatoes are so often turned into sauce or enjoyed raw that the virtues of roasting them are often overlooked. Here they're sweet and juicy with the lovely rich hint of saffron. This is a wonderful side to serve with rice or grains to soak up the juices.

SERVES: 6–8
PREPARATION: 10 minutes
COOKING: 15 minutes

60 ml (2 fl oz/¼ cup) olive oil
1 large pinch saffron threads, crushed
1 pinch sweet paprika
1 pinch allspice
8 ripe tomatoes, about 1 kg (2 lb 4 oz), sliced in half horizontally

250 g (9 oz) silken tofu
2 teaspoons finely grated lemon zest
sea salt flakes
freshly ground black pepper
1 small handful mixed herbs like parsley, mint, chives, oregano, chopped

Heat the oven to 180°C (350°F/Gas 4). Mix the oil, saffron and spices together in a small pan and warm over a gentle heat until aromatic.

Heat 2 tablespoons of the saffron-infused oil in an ovenproof frying pan and add the tomatoes, cut-side down. Cook over a medium–high heat for about 3 minutes, or until starting to take on some colour. Turn the tomatoes over and cook for a few minutes more. Transfer the frying pan to the oven and roast for about 10 minutes until very tender.

Meanwhile, whisk together the tofu, lemon zest and salt and pepper. Add the herbs and gently stir to combine.

Serve the tomatoes drizzled with the remaining saffron-infused oil with spoonfuls of the herbed tofu on top.

stuffed capsicums

WITH CUMIN POTATOES

These capsicums have bags of flavour thanks to the delicious combination of herbs and spices. The pomegranate molasses adds extra depth of flavour.

SERVES: 4–6 as a side
PREPARATION: 20 minutes
COOKING: about 45 minutes

2 teaspoons black onion seeds
1 tablespoon pomegranate molasses
3 tablespoons rapeseed or vegetable oil
500 g (1 lb 2 oz) all-purpose potatoes such as desiree, peeled and cut into 1.5 cm (⅝ inch) dice
1½ teaspoons ground cumin
1 teaspoon sweet smoked paprika
1 teaspoon garam masala

sea salt flakes
freshly ground black pepper
60 g (2¼ oz) silverbeet (Swiss chard), shredded
3 tablespoons unsweetened soya yoghurt
3–4 capsicums (peppers) of various colours
olive oil, for drizzling
1 small handful chopped coriander (cilantro), for sprinkling

Toast the onion seeds in a dry frying pan until fragrant, about 2 minutes. Set aside.

In a small bowl, whisk together the pomegranate molasses and 3 tablespoons water. Set aside.

Heat the oil in a large frying pan over a medium–high heat and add the potatoes. Cook, constantly turning the potatoes over, for about 5 minutes. Add the cumin, paprika, garam masala, onion seeds and salt and pepper. Continue cooking and turning until the potatoes are golden and only just tender. Add the silverbeet and toss until wilted. Add the pomegranate molasses mixture, scraping the bottom of the pan as it bubbles up, and cook until the liquid is absorbed and the potatoes are glossy. Remove from the heat and gently stir through the yoghurt. Taste for seasoning.

Heat the oven to 180°C (350°F/Gas 4). Cut the capsicums in half lengthways and carefully remove the seeds and white membrane without damaging the flesh. Arrange cut-side up in an ovenproof dish or baking tray. Distribute the potato mixture among the capsicums and drizzle with olive oil. Bake for 30 minutes. Serve hot or at room temperature, sprinkled with coriander.

warm potato salad

WITH PISTACHIO BUTTER DRESSING

Everyone loves potato salad but sometimes the traditional mayonnaise dressing is a bit stodgy. This dressing is lighter and tastier.

SERVES: 4 as a side
PREPARATION: 20 minutes
COOKING: 15 minutes

800 g (1 lb 12 oz) charlotte or other all-purpose potatoes, halved
fine sea salt
100 g (3½ oz) shelled pistachio nuts
1 garlic clove, finely chopped

3 tablespoons vegetable oil
3 tablespoons lemon juice
sea salt flakes
freshly ground black pepper
1 handful basil leaves, torn

Cook the potatoes in boiling salted water until tender. Be careful not to overcook.

Meanwhile, blitz the pistachio nuts in a food processor to a smooth butter. This might take longer than you think; just keep processing until creamy. (You will have more butter than necessary for the dressing, but use the excess in another recipe or spread on hot toast.)

In a small bowl, whisk 2 tablespoons of the pistachio butter with the garlic, oil, lemon juice and salt and pepper. Taste and adjust the seasoning or lemon juice.

While the potatoes are still warm, gently toss with the pistachio dressing and the basil leaves. Serve warm.

roasted tofu

WITH AFRICAN SPICES

This is packed full of flavour yet requires almost no work. The key is to press the tofu properly to drain away as much water as possible. This works very well served with a bowl of grains like barley or farro.

SERVES: 4 as a side
PREPARATION: 10 minutes, plus 20 minutes pressing
COOKING: 40 minutes

grated zest of 1 orange
150 ml (5 fl oz) vegetable stock
1 tablespoon agave nectar
3 tablespoons lime juice
2 tablespoons olive oil
2 garlic cloves, crushed
1 tablespoon ground cumin
½ tablespoon ground cinnamon
½ tablespoon allspice

½ tablespoon smoked paprika
½ teaspoon fine sea salt
¾ teaspoon cayenne pepper
¾ teaspoon turmeric
freshly ground black pepper
500 g (1 lb 2 oz) firm tofu, pressed (*see* p 15)
finely sliced spring onions (scallions),
to serve (optional)

Heat the oven to 220°C (425°F/Gas 7). Whisk together all the ingredients except the tofu and spring onions.

Cut the pressed tofu into 16 equal pieces. Put in a single layer in a shallow ovenproof dish. Cover with the marinade and gently turn each piece over to coat on all sides. Roast for 20 minutes, then flip the tofu over and cook for 20 minutes more. A lot of the marinade will have been absorbed. Remove the tofu pieces to a serving plate and sprinkle with the spring onions (if using). Serve immediately.

stuffed artichokes

WITH GARLICKY BREADCRUMBS

Don't be deterred if you haven't cooked artichokes before – this dish is very easy and the results impressive. Only buy the freshest artichokes that have compact, firm leaves.

SERVES: 4–6
PREPARATION: 30 minutes
COOKING: about 1 hour

165 g (5¾ oz) breadcrumbs
100 g (3½ oz) vegan parmesan cheese, home-made (*see* p 102) or grated shop-bought
3 tablespoons chopped flat-leaf (Italian) parsley
3 tablespoons chopped sage
3 tablespoons chopped mint
juice and grated zest of 1 lemon

2 teaspoons sea salt flakes
1 teaspoon freshly ground black pepper
1 red chilli, seeded and finely sliced
5 garlic cloves, finely chopped
250 ml (9 fl oz/1 cup) olive oil
8 medium artichokes
200 ml (7 fl oz) vegan white wine

Heat the oven to 220°C (425°F/Gas 7). In a large bowl, stir together the breadcrumbs, three-quarters of the parmesan cheese, the parsley, sage, mint, lemon zest, salt, pepper, chilli, garlic and 60 ml (2 fl oz/¼ cup) of the olive oil.

Fill a bowl with cold water and add the lemon juice. Slice off the top one-third of each artichoke using a serrated knife and discard. Pull off the tough outer leaves – it might seem like you are discarding too much of the artichoke, but only the tender centre is enjoyable to eat. Cut off the stems so the artichokes sit flat. Put in the lemon water to prevent browning.

Working with one artichoke at a time, pat dry with paper towels and open out the leaves a little. Stuff the gaps with some of the breadcrumb mixture. Put in an ovenproof dish. Repeat. Drizzle with the remaining oil. Pour the white wine into the dish and add enough water to come 2 cm (¾ inch) up the sides. Cover tightly with foil and bake for about 1 hour, or until a skewer slides into the base of an artichoke easily. Sprinkle with the remaining parmesan and put under a hot grill (broiler) for a few minutes until golden. Serve immediately.

creamed greens

Steamed, boiled or sautéed vegetables are all well and good, but sometimes something more comforting is called for. This is it.

SERVES: 4 as a side
PREPARATION: 10 minutes, once the cashew cream is made
COOKING: about 20 minutes

4 tablespoons olive oil
200 g (7 oz) trimmed and sliced greens such as baby English spinach, kale or silverbeet (Swiss chard)
1 onion, diced
2 garlic cloves, finely chopped
200 ml (7 fl oz) vegetable stock
300 ml (10½ fl oz) unsweetened non-dairy milk

2 tablespoons lemon juice
2 tablespoons nutritional yeast
¼ teaspoon grated nutmeg
sea salt flakes
freshly ground black pepper
4 tablespoons cashew cream (*see* p 26)

Heat 2 tablespoons of the oil in a frying pan and sauté the greens over a medium–high heat until tender. Remove to a bowl.

Wipe out the pan, heat the remaining olive oil and cook the onion until tender, about 7 minutes. Add the garlic and cook for 2 minutes more. Add the stock, milk, lemon juice, nutritional yeast, nutmeg and salt and pepper. Gently simmer for 5 minutes, or until thickened slightly. Transfer to a blender,

add the cashew cream and blitz until smooth and creamy. Return to the pan, add the greens and stir over a medium–low heat until the sauce has thickened and reduced. Serve hot.

potatoes dauphinoise

My family, avid fans of potatoes dauphinoise made with milk, cream and cheese, attest to the success of this dish: they love it. The almond milk and cashew cream combine to make such a divinely rich and creamy sauce that the absence of dairy isn't an issue at all.

SERVES: 4 as a side
PREPARATION: 10 minutes
COOKING: 40 minutes

350 ml (12 fl oz) unsweetened almond milk, plus more for thinning if needed
250 ml (9 fl oz/1 cup) cashew cream (*see* p 26) diluted with 100 ml (3½ fl oz) vegetable stock or water
1 splash vegan white wine
2 garlic cloves, finely chopped
1 thyme sprig
1 bay leaf
½ onion, peeled
sea salt flakes
freshly ground black pepper
600 g (1 lb 5 oz) potatoes, boiling potatoes are best, such as Dutch cream
vegetable oil, for oiling
2 tablespoons nutritional yeast

Heat the oven to 200°C (400°F/Gas 6). Mix the milk, diluted cream, wine, garlic, thyme, bay leaf, onion and salt and pepper together in a pan and simmer for about 5 minutes.

Meanwhile, peel and finely slice the potatoes, ideally using a mandoline. Slide the potatoes into the milk mixture, stir and simmer until almost tender — they will finish cooking in the oven.

Lightly oil an ovenproof dish. When the potatoes are cooked, remove them from the milk with a slotted spoon and transfer to the ovenproof dish.

Strain the milk mixture to catch the thyme, onion and bay leaf and pour enough of the milk over the potatoes to just cover — you might not need all of it. (The milk should be the consistency of thin cream. If it has thickened too much while simmering add a little extra milk or water.)

Sprinkle over the nutritional yeast. Put the ovenproof dish on a baking tray and bake for about 30 minutes, or until bubbling and golden and the potatoes are tender. Leave to stand for a few minutes before serving.

patatas bravas

This is a rich, spicy and wonderfully tasty dish that
works brilliantly as part of a mezze spread.

SERVES: 4
PREPARATION: 15 minutes
COOKING: 40 minutes

**1 litre (35 fl oz/4 cups) vegetable oil,
for deep-frying**
**900 g (2 lb) boiling potatoes, peeled, halved
and each half quartered**
½ teaspoon fine sea salt
3 tablespoons olive oil
1 large onion, finely chopped
**60 g (2¼ oz) piquillo peppers, or other roasted
red capsicums (peppers), chopped**
2 garlic cloves, finely chopped

**600 ml (12 fl oz) tomato passata
(puréed tomatoes)**
1 large pinch caster (superfine) sugar
1 tablespoon sweet smoked paprika
½ teaspoon cayenne pepper
1 bay leaf
sea salt flakes
freshly ground black pepper

Heat the vegetable oil in a large pan. Sprinkle the
potatoes with salt and very gently simmer in the
oil for 15 minutes until tender but not coloured.
Drain and reserve the oil.

Heat the olive oil in a pan and gently fry the onion
and peppers or capsicums over a low heat for
10 minutes until soft and sweet. Add the garlic
and cook for 5 minutes more. Add the tomato
passata, sugar, paprika, cayenne and bay leaf and
simmer to a thick sauce. Season well with salt
and pepper, remove the bay leaf and set aside.

Reheat the reserved oil until very hot and quickly
fry the potatoes until golden. Remove from the oil
with a slotted spoon. Serve immediately, with the
sauce spooned over.

CHAPTER 6

pasta, rice & noodles

+++

rich mushroom lasagne

This is very rich and delicious. Make sure the béchamel is not too thick before you assemble the lasagne. If it is, just add a little water or more of the porcini liquor to loosen. Serve with a crisp green salad.

SERVES: 4–6
PREPARATION: 30 minutes, plus 20 minutes soaking
COOKING: about 1 hour

40 g (1½ oz) dried porcini mushrooms
400 g (14 oz) vegan lasagne sheets
3 tablespoons refined coconut oil
or non-dairy butter
800 g (1 lb 12 oz) mixed fresh mushrooms, sliced
2 garlic cloves, finely chopped
1 generous squeeze lemon juice
2 tablespoons chopped tarragon
4 tablespoons chopped flat-leaf (Italian) parsley
sea salt flakes
freshly ground black pepper

200 ml (7 fl oz) cashew cream (see p 26) diluted with
100 ml (3½ fl oz) vegan white wine or water
3 tablespoons nutritional yeast

FOR THE BÉCHAMEL SAUCE
750 ml (26 fl oz/3 cups) unsweetened non-dairy milk
75 g non-dairy butter
50 g (1¾ oz/⅓ cups) plain (all-purpose) flour
1 pinch ground nutmeg
sea salt flakes
1 pinch white pepper

Cover the porcini mushrooms with boiling water and soak for 20 minutes. Drain, reserve the soaking liquor and squeeze out excess liquid. Chop and set aside. Meanwhile, pour boiling water over the lasagne sheets and soak for 2 minutes. Drain and spread out in a single layer on paper towels or clean tea towels (dish towels).

Heat the oil or butter in a frying pan and add the fresh mushrooms, the porcini mushrooms and garlic. Cook, stirring, until the mushrooms are tender and releasing their juices. Add the squeeze of lemon juice, 3 tablespoons of the reserved porcini liquor, the tarragon, parsley and salt and pepper. Stir. There should be a couple of tablespoons of juices in the pan. If not, add a splash more porcini liquor. Set aside.

To make the béchamel, bring the milk to the boil. Meanwhile, stir the butter and flour together in

a pan over a medium heat. Remove from the heat and gradually add the hot milk, stirring constantly, making sure each addition is absorbed before adding the next. Return to the heat, add the nutmeg and season with salt and the white pepper. Cook, stirring, until the sauce is the consistency of thin custard. Add a little water if needed. Set aside.

Heat the oven to 180°C (350°F/Gas 4). Pour one-quarter of the béchamel into a 35 x 25 cm (14 x 10 inch) ovenproof dish. Add a single layer of lasagne sheets. Spread half the mushroom mixture on top, sprinkle with 1 tablespoon of the nutritional yeast and spoon over half the diluted cashew cream. Repeat, finishing with nutritional yeast.

Bake for 30–40 minutes, or until the sauce is bubbling, the top golden and the lasagne sheets tender.

sweet potato ravioli

WITH SAGE BUTTER & PINE NUTS

This delicate pasta wrapped around a sweet and tasty filling makes
a special dinner that's worth the little bit of effort involved.

SERVES: 2 as a main or 4 as a starter
PREPARATION: 1 hour, including making the pasta dough
COOKING: about 1 hour

1 quantity pasta dough (*see* p 32)
2 medium sweet potatoes, about 375 g (13 oz)
2 tablespoons olive oil
1 small white onion, finely chopped
2 garlic cloves, finely chopped
1 tablespoon breadcrumbs
1 tablespoon nutritional yeast
1 pinch ground nutmeg

¼ teaspoon chilli powder, or more to taste
sea salt flakes
freshly ground black pepper
plain (all-purpose) flour, for dusting
3 tablespoons non-dairy butter
10 small sage leaves
2 tablespoons pine nuts

Start by making the pasta (*see* p 32). While the
dough is resting, make the rest of the dish.

Set the oven to 180°C (350°F/Gas 4). Put the
sweet potatoes on a baking tray and roast for
about 40 minutes. The exact time will vary
according to the size of the potatoes, so check
after 30 minutes. A sharp knife or skewer will
slide in easily when done. Slice open to cool.

Meanwhile, heat the oil in a frying pan and gently
fry the onion until soft, about 8 minutes. Add the
garlic and cook for 2 minutes more. Set aside.
Scoop the sweet potato flesh into a bowl and
stir in the onion, breadcrumbs, nutritional yeast,
nutmeg, chilli powder and salt and pepper. Add
more salt, pepper or chilli powder to taste.

Roll out the dough into sheets 2 mm (¹⁄₁₆ inch)
thick. Stamp out 40 circles with an 8 cm (3¼ inch)
round cookie cutter and transfer to a floured board.
Dampen the edges of a pasta circle with water.
Put a teaspoon of the sweet potato mixture in the
centre, put another pasta circle on top and press
the edges together tightly, squeezing out any air,
to seal. Set aside on a floured board. Repeat.

Drop the ravioli into a pan of simmering salted
water and cook for 3 minutes, or until they rise
to the top. Remove with a slotted spoon and set
aside. Meanwhile, fry the butter, sage and pine
nuts until the leaves start to crisp. Be careful not
to burn them. Serve the ravioli in shallow bowls
with the buttery sage leaves and the pine nuts
spooned over.

fusilli

WITH ARTICHOKE CREAM

This is designed to use the home-made cream cheese on p 103. You can use a shop-bought version, but if you do, make sure that when you whisk together the cream cheese and stock you end up with about 500 ml (17 fl oz/2 cups) of liquid.

+++ +++

SERVES: 4
PREPARATION: 10 minutes, once the cream cheese is made
COOKING: 20 minutes

200 g (7 oz) non-dairy cream cheese (*see* p 103)
200 ml (7 fl oz) mild vegetable stock, or more if needed
300 g (10½ oz) artichokes in oil (drained weight), chopped
1 garlic clove, finely chopped
2 tablespoons lemon juice, or more or less to taste

sea salt flakes
freshly ground black pepper
500 g (1 lb 2 oz) vegan fusilli or pasta shells
olive oil, for tossing
16 cherry tomatoes, halved
2 tablespoons chopped chives or flat-leaf (Italian) parsley

In a small pan, whisk together the cream cheese and stock over a gentle heat to make a creamy sauce. Add the artichokes and garlic and simmer very gently for about 10 minutes, stirring occasionally. Transfer to a blender and blitz to a smooth sauce. Wipe out the pan, pour the sauce back in and add lemon juice to taste. Add a little more stock if too thick. Season with salt and pepper and set aside to keep warm.

Meanwhile, cook the pasta in boiling salted water following the packet directions, or until just *al dente*. Drain, toss with a little olive oil and return to the pan. Stir through the artichoke cream, the tomatoes and most of the chives or parsley. Serve immediately, sprinkled with the remaining chives or parsley.

carbonara-style spaghetti

WITH CRISPY SHIITAKE BACON

My 12-year-old daughter, who normally detests mushrooms and adores
traditional carbonara pasta in all its eggy, cheesy glory,
loves this version. Enough said.

SERVES: 2
PREPARATION: 15 minutes, once the cashew cream is made
COOKING: 25 minutes

FOR THE SHIITAKE BACON
sea salt flakes
freshly ground black pepper
2 teaspoons smoked paprika
8 drops liquid smoke* (optional)
1 teaspoon garlic powder
1 teaspoon onion powder
1 tablespoon vegetable oil
100 g (3½ oz) shiitake mushrooms, sliced

FOR THE SAUCE & PASTA
250 g (9 oz) vegan spaghetti
fine sea salt
olive oil, for tossing
200 ml (7 fl oz) porcini mushroom or
vegetable stock
1½ teaspoons white miso paste
1 teaspoon garlic granules
1 teaspoon onion granules
125 ml (4 fl oz/½ cup) cashew cream (*see* p 26)
freshly ground black pepper
2 tablespoons chopped flat-leaf (Italian) parsley,
to serve (optional)

Heat the oven to 170°C (325°F/Gas 3). Line a
baking tray with baking paper. Combine all the
bacon ingredients except the mushrooms in a
mixing bowl. Add the mushrooms and toss to
coat. Spread out in a single layer on the prepared
baking tray and roast for 7–10 minutes until
sizzling and golden. Set aside to cool.

Cook the pasta in boiling salted water following
the packet directions. Drain and return to the pan.
Toss with a little olive oil and set aside. While the
pasta is cooking, make the sauce. In a small pan,
heat the stock, then whisk in the miso paste until

dissolved. Reduce the heat and add the garlic and
onion granules, the cashew cream and salt and
pepper. Stir constantly for about 5 minutes until
the mixture thickens into a creamy sauce. Taste
for seasoning – the sauce might need quite a bit
of salt.

Toss the pasta and sauce together and stir through
the shiitake. Distribute into bowls, ensuring each
receives equal amounts of the shiitake. Serve
sprinkled with the parsley (if using).

*A smoky flavouring available at some supermarkets
and online.

coriander & peanut pesto

WITH PENNE

Traditional basil pesto is often left a little chunky for texture, but this version is blitzed smooth so the peanuts turn creamy. You will probably have leftover pesto but it keeps well in the fridge, covered, for a couple of days.

SERVES: 4 with pesto left over
PREPARATION: 10 minutes
COOKING: about 8 minutes

400 g (14 oz) vegan penne
fine sea salt
olive oil, for tossing
55 g (2 oz) coriander (cilantro) leaves, plus extra, chopped, to serve
125 g (4½ oz) unsalted peanuts, toasted, plus extra chopped, to serve

150 ml (5 fl oz) vegetable oil
1 garlic clove
1 green chilli, seeded, finely sliced, plus extra to serve (optional)
juice of 2 limes
sea salt flakes
freshly ground black pepper

Cook the pasta in boiling salted water following the packet directions. Meanwhile, blitz the coriander leaves, peanuts, vegetable oil, garlic, chilli and lime juice to a smooth paste in a blender. Season to taste with salt and pepper, adding more lime juice if needed.

When the pasta is cooked, scoop out a little of the cooking water and set aside. Drain the pasta, then return it to the pan. Stir through 4 heaped tablespoons of the pesto to coat, adding a little of the reserved cooking water to loosen if needed. Serve into bowls and top with a spoonful more pesto. Sprinkle with the chopped coriander, peanuts and sliced chilli (if using).

macaroni & cheese

Creamy and delicious, this version of the comfort food classic is a winner with omnivores, so it must be good. I like to add peas for colour and freshness but feel free to omit the greenery if you're a purist.

SERVES: 4–6
PREPARATION: 20 minutes
COOKING: 35 minutes, once the cheese sauce is made

300 g (10½ oz) macaroni or small tube pasta
fine sea salt
150 g (5½ oz) ciabatta or sourdough, torn
1 tablespoon nutritional yeast
2 tablespoons olive oil, plus extra for tossing

60 g (2¼ oz) frozen peas
1 pinch paprika
2 quantities cheese sauce (*see* p 103), warm
about 60 ml (2 fl oz/¼ cup) vegetable stock, if needed
non-dairy butter, for greasing

Cook the macaroni in boiling salted water following the packet directions. Drain, rinse in cold water and toss with a little olive oil. Set aside.

Heat the oven to 180°C (350°F/Gas 4). Meanwhile, put the bread in a blender or food processor, add the nutritional yeast and the olive oil. Blitz to a breadcrumb consistency. Set aside. Blanch the peas in boiling salted water.

In a large bowl, gently toss together the pasta, the cheese sauce, peas and paprika. There should be lots of sauce so if the mixture is too thick, stir in some or all of the stock. Grease a shallow ovenproof dish approximately 25 x 17 cm (10 x 6½ inches) with butter. Tip in the pasta and sprinkle with the breadcrumb topping. Bake for about 25 minutes, or until the cheese sauce is bubbling and the top golden.

roast cauliflower risotto

WITH TAHINI CREAM

This is a rich and delicious way to cook cauliflower, and very
filling. Serve with a green salad.

SERVES: 4
PREPARATION: 20 minutes
COOKING: 40 minutes

FOR THE CAULIFLOWER
60 ml (2 fl oz/¼ cup) olive oil
60 ml (2 fl oz/¼ cup) balsamic vinegar
4 garlic cloves, crushed
2 teaspoons dried thyme
½ teaspoon sea salt flakes
freshly ground black pepper
450 g (1 lb) cauliflower florets, cut small

FOR THE TAHINI CREAM
70 g (2½ oz) tahini paste
1 tablespoon chopped mint
1 tablespoon chopped flat-leaf (Italian) parsley,
plus extra leaves to serve

150 g (5½ oz) soya yoghurt
finely grated zest of 1 lemon
2 tablespoons lemon juice
1 teaspoon pomegranate molasses
2 tablespoons warm water

FOR THE RISOTTO
1.25–1.5 litres (44–52 fl oz/5–6 cups) vegetable
stock (*see* p 34)
3 tablespoons olive oil
1 large onion, finely chopped
400 g (14 oz) arborio or carnaroli rice
100 ml (3½ fl oz) vegan white wine

Heat the oven to 220°C (425°F/Gas 7). Line a large
baking tray with baking paper. In a mixing bowl,
whisk all the cauliflower ingredients together
except the cauliflower. Spread the cauliflower out
in the baking tray, pour over the dressing and toss
to coat. Roast for 25 minutes, or until starting to
char at the edges. Set aside.

Meanwhile, for the tahini cream, mix all the
ingredients together until smooth and creamy.
Set aside.

To make the risotto, heat the stock and set over
a low heat to keep hot. Heat the oil in a large
heavy pan, add the onion and cook until soft but

not coloured. Add the rice, stir well and cook a
little to lightly toast. Add the wine and stir until
evaporated. Add the stock 1 ladleful at a time,
stirring between each addition. Ensure each
ladleful is absorbed before adding the next. The
rice is cooked when the grains are tender but
retain some bite. The mixture should still be quite
wet when cooked so stir in more stock if too dry.

Remove from the heat and stir through the tahini
cream and half the cauliflower. Let the pan sit with
the lid on for 2 minutes. Stir well before spooning
into bowls. Top with the remaining cauliflower and
sprinkle with the parsley leaves.

risotto primavera

No plate of food shouts springtime as deliciously as this one – although you can, of course, make it with frozen veg any time of the year. Good-quality stock is key so try to use home-made (*see* p 34) rather than ready-made.

SERVES: 4
PREPARATION: 15 minutes
COOKING: 30 minutes

1.25 litres (44 fl oz/5 cups) vegetable stock
250 g (9 oz) young asparagus spears, woody ends snapped off
200 g (7 oz) shelled broad beans, fresh or frozen
150 g (5½ oz) peas, fresh or frozen
3 tablespoons olive oil, plus extra for drizzling
4 shallots, finely chopped

400 g (14 oz) arborio or carnaroli rice
100 ml (3½ fl oz) white vermouth or vegan white wine
finely grated zest of 1 lemon
2 tablespoon chopped mint
4 heaped tablespoons vegan parmesan cheese, home-made (*see* p 102) or grated shop-bought

Bring the vegetable stock to a simmer in a large pan. Cut each asparagus spear into 4 pieces and add to the stock. Cook for 2 minutes, or until almost tender, then remove with a slotted spoon and set aside. Blanch the broad beans and peas in the same way. Remove and set aside with the asparagus. Keep the stock hot over a low heat.

Heat the oil in a large pan and gently fry the shallots for 3 minutes, or until soft but not coloured. Add the rice and stir for 1 minute to lightly toast and coat in the oil. Add the vermouth or wine and stir until evaporated. Set the timer for

20 minutes and start to add the stock, 1 ladleful at a time, stirring between each addition. Make sure each ladleful is absorbed before adding the next.

After 15 minutes, stir the vegetables into the rice and continue to add the stock as before. Taste the rice – the mixture should be quite wet and the grains tender but retaining some bite. When cooked, remove from the heat and stir in the lemon zest, mint and parmesan cheese. Taste for seasoning, then leave to rest with the lid on for 2 minutes. Give the rice a good stir before ladling into bowls. Serve drizzled with olive oil.

gnocchi

WITH TRUFFLED CAULIFLOWER SAUCE

If you're going to make your own gnocchi – and it is worth the effort – it might as well be a bit of a treat. This recipe is decadent and delicious, especially if you add a sprinkling of truffle shavings at the end.

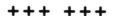

SERVES: 4
PREPARATION: 45 minutes
COOKING: about 2 hours 10 minutes

FOR THE SAUCE
400 g (14 oz) cauliflower florets, cut small
1 onion, quartered
1 garlic bulb, separated into cloves, skin on
2 tablespoons rapeseed or vegetable oil
sea salt flakes
2 teaspoons truffle oil, or more to taste
250 ml (9 fl oz/1 cup) unsweetened non-dairy milk, plus extra if needed
300 ml (10½ fl oz) vegetable stock, plus extra if needed

freshly ground black pepper
shaved black or white truffle, to serve (optional)

FOR THE GNOCCHI
1 kg (2 lb 4 oz) all-purpose potatoes, ideally desiree, pricked all over with a fork
200 g (7 oz) plain (all-purpose) flour, ideally 00, plus extra for dusting
½ teaspoon fine sea salt
1 pinch nutmeg

Heat the oven to 190°C (375°F/Gas 5). In a baking tray, toss the cauliflower, onion and garlic in the rapeseed or vegetable oil and sprinkle with salt. Roast for 45 minutes, or until tender. Shake the tray a couple of times during cooking. Set aside when cooked, then bake the potatoes for 1 hour–1 hour 15 minutes, or until very soft.

Meanwhile, put the cauliflower, onion, the flesh from the garlic cloves, truffle oil, milk, stock and salt and pepper in a blender and blitz until smooth. Transfer to a pan and gently heat, adding more stock or milk if too thick. Keep warm.

While the potatoes are hot, scoop out the flesh and push through a potato ricer or sieve into

a mound on a work surface dusted with flour. Sprinkle over the salt and nutmeg. Gradually knead in the flour to make a soft dough.

Tear off a lemon-sized piece of dough and roll into a sausage shape 3 cm (1¼ inches) in diameter. Cut at 3 cm (1¼ inch) intervals to make square pillows. Set aside on a floured tray. Repeat. Press indentations in the gnocchi with the tines of a fork.

Cook the gnocchi in gently simmering salted water until they bob to the surface. Tip into a serving dish and stir through the sauce. Serve immediately, sprinkled with the shaved truffle (if using).

bolognese sauce

This is a lovely alternative to meat-based bolognese sauce.

SERVES: 4–6
PREPARATION: 20 minutes
COOKING: 50 minutes

3 tablespoons olive oil, plus extra for tossing
1 onion, diced small
1 carrot, diced small
1 celery stalk, diced small
1 star anise
2 garlic cloves, finely chopped
150 g (5½ oz) puy lentils or tiny blue-green lentils, rinsed
200 ml (7 fl oz) vegan red wine
2 tablespoons tomato paste (concentrated purée)

1 x 400 g (14 oz) tin chopped tomatoes
15 g (½ oz) miso paste (optional)
2 teaspoons sea salt flakes
1 chipotle (optional)
2 bay leaves
1 x 400 g (14 oz) tinned adzuki, borlotti or kidney beans, drained
500 g (1 lb 2 oz) vegan tagliatelle
fine sea salt
basil leaves, torn, to serve (optional)

Heat the oil in a large pan and gently fry the onion, carrot, celery and star anise until soft and starting to caramelise, about 10 minutes. Don't shortcut this step as cooking the vegetables slowly is important. Add the garlic and cook for a few minutes more.

Stir in the lentils, then add the wine, scraping the bottom of the pan with a spoon as it bubbles up. Add the tomato paste and stir over a medium heat until the wine has evaporated and the paste starts to smell fragrant.

Add the tomatoes, miso paste (if using) and salt. Stir. Don't worry that this seems like a lot of salt as lentils and beans require hefty seasoning. Tuck the chipotle (if using) and bay leaves into the

sauce. Bring to the boil then reduce the heat and simmer, uncovered, for 40 minutes, or until the lentils are tender. Add more water if the mixture starts drying out. Stir occasionally.

When the lentils are cooked, add the beans and gently simmer to warm through. Meanwhile, cook the pasta in boiling salted water following the packet directions. Drain, return to the pan and toss with a splash of olive oil. Set aside.

Remove the bay leaves, star anise and chipotle from the sauce. Add a couple of ladlefuls of sauce to the pasta and gently toss to coat. Serve the pasta into shallow bowls and spoon more sauce on top. Serve scattered with basil leaves (if using).

saffron couscous

WITH VEGETABLES & PINE NUTS

This is a wonderfully fragrant and
delicious side dish or substantial main.

SERVES: 4
PREPARATION: 20 minutes
COOKING: 35 minutes

2 tablespoons olive oil
1/2 onion, chopped
**1 x 400 g (14 oz) tinned chickpeas,
drained and rinsed**
**1 large carrot, quartered lengthways and
chopped into 1 cm (1/2 inch) pieces**
**1/4 butternut pumpkin (squash), peeled and
cut into 1 cm (1/2 inch) dice**
**1/2 zucchini (courgette), quartered lengthways
and cut into 1 cm (1/2 inch) pieces**
700 ml (24 fl oz) vegetable stock

1 generous pinch saffron threads, crushed
sea salt flakes
freshly ground black pepper
140 g (5 oz) couscous
2 tablespoons sultanas
20 g (3/4 oz) pitted dates, chopped
1/2 teaspoon ground cinnamon
1–2 tablespoons pine nuts
1 tablespoon granulated sugar

Heat 1 tablespoon of the oil in a pan and cook
the onion until soft and golden, about 10 minutes.
Add the chickpeas, carrot, pumpkin and zucchini
and stir to coat in the oil. Add the stock and
saffron, season with salt and pepper and bring
to the boil. Reduce the heat and simmer until the
vegetables are just tender, 8–10 minutes. Drain
the vegetables, reserving the stock, and set aside.
Return the stock to the pan and keep hot.

In a bowl, cover the couscous with 375 ml (13 fl oz/
1 1/2 cups) of the reserved stock, cover with plastic
wrap and set aside for 5–10 minutes until tender.
Fluff with a fork.

In a shallow ovenproof dish, combine the couscous,
cooked vegetables, sultanas, dates, cinnamon and
the remaining olive oil. Taste for seasoning and
add more salt if needed. Scatter the pine nuts on
top, then sprinkle over the sugar. Cook under a
hot grill (broiler) until the nuts are golden, about
5 minutes. Serve immediately.

marinated tempeh & sesame noodles

Tempeh has a lovely chewy quality that's very moreish in this spicy noodle dish.

SERVES: 4 as a side
PREPARATION: 10 minutes
COOKING: about 12 minutes

60 ml (2 fl oz/¼ cup) light soy sauce
2 tablespoons rice vinegar
2 cm (¾ inch) piece fresh ginger, peeled and finely grated
1 garlic clove, grated
2 teaspoons agave nectar
225 g (8 oz) tempeh, cut into thin bite-sized slices
200 g (7 oz) medium rice noodles
1 splash sesame oil
175 g (6 oz) snow peas (mangetout)
fine sea salt
2 tablespoons vegetable oil
1 handful coriander (cilantro), chopped

FOR THE SESAME DRESSING
2 tablespoons tahini paste
100 ml (3½ fl oz) vegetable oil
1 large garlic clove
1 teaspoon onion granules
1 tablespoon toasted sesame oil
2 tablespoons soy sauce
60 ml (2 fl oz/¼ cup) rice vinegar
2 tablespoons soft light brown sugar
1 teaspoon hot chilli paste
2 tablespoons chopped coriander (cilantro)
90 ml (3 fl oz) hot water

Whisk together the soy, vinegar, ginger, garlic, agave and 1 tablespoon water. Put the tempeh slices in a shallow bowl and pour over the marinade. Set aside for at least 30 minutes.

Meanwhile, cook the noodles following the packet directions. Drain, toss with the sesame oil and set aside. Blanch the snow peas in boiling salted water, drain and refresh in cold water. Set aside.

To make the dressing, blitz the ingredients together in a blender until smooth and creamy. Set aside.

Heat the vegetable oil until very hot in a heavy frying pan and stir-fry the tempeh until brown on all sides. Add the drained noodles and snow peas and toss to warm through. Remove to a serving plate and toss with the dressing. Serve immediately, sprinkled with the coriander.

toasted cashew nut fried rice

WITH SILVERBEET

Children love this dish as rice is always a winner, and it's a great
way to encourage them to eat nuts and green vegetables.

SERVES: 4 as a side
PREPARATION: 10 minutes
COOKING: 20 minutes

200 g (7 oz/1 cup) basmati rice
1 pinch fine sea salt
3 tablespoons olive oil
1 teaspoon mustard seeds
100 g (3½ oz) raw cashew nuts
1 onion, thinly sliced
2 garlic cloves, finely chopped

1 red chilli, seeded and finely chopped,
plus extra to serve (optional)
60 g (2¼ oz) trimmed silverbeet
(Swiss or rainbow chard), shredded
finely grated zest of 1 lemon
sea salt flakes
freshly ground black pepper

Lightly toast the rice in a dry lidded pan until
aromatic. Stir in the salt, 1 tablespoon of the olive
oil and 500 ml (17 fl oz/2 cups) water. Bring to the
boil, cover and reduce the heat to low. Very gently
cook for 15 minutes, then remove from the heat
and set aside for 5 minutes with the lid on.

Meanwhile, heat the remaining oil in a frying pan
and fry the mustard seeds for 30 seconds. Add the
cashew nuts and stir-fry for 30 seconds more. Add
the onion and cook over a medium heat, stirring

constantly, until golden and caramelised, about
10 minutes. Add the garlic and chilli and cook for
3 minutes more. Finally, add the silverbeet and
cook until wilted.

Fluff the rice with a fork and tip into a shallow
serving dish. Gently fork through the onion,
silverbeet and most of the lemon zest. Taste
for seasoning and add more salt and pepper if
needed. Sprinkle with the remaining lemon zest
and chilli (if using). Serve hot.

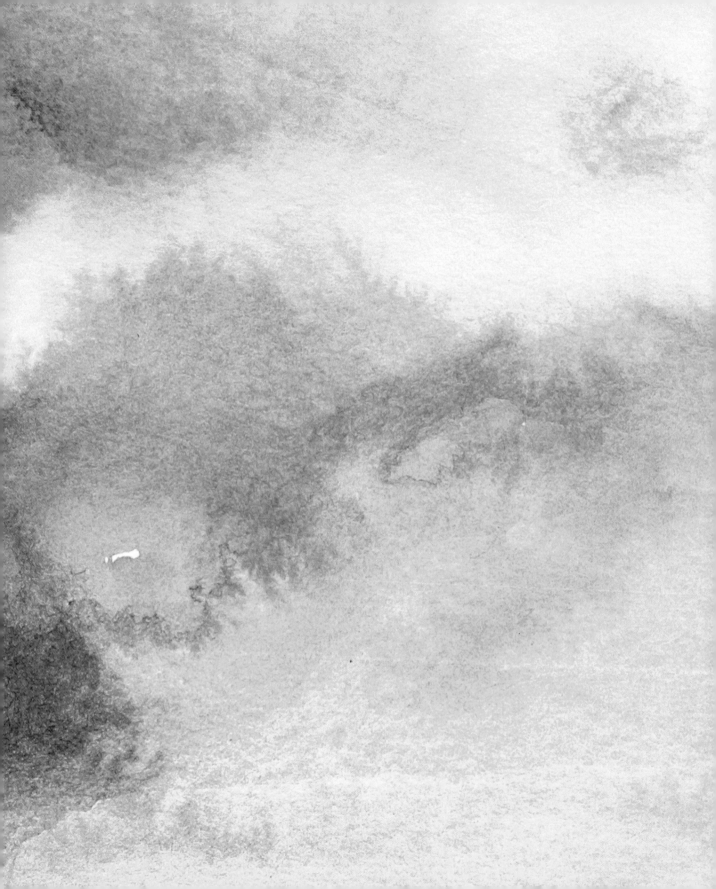

CHAPTER 7

warming mains

+ + +

sweet potato & beetroot gratin

There's something cheering about cutting into this gratin to reveal its vibrant orange and red interior. A bowl of steamed greens on the side would make this a healthful, not to mention colourful, main meal.

SERVES: 4–6
PREPARATION: 20 minutes, plus 20 minutes marinating
COOKING: about 50 minutes

vegetable oil, for oiling
2 sweet potatoes, about 450 g (1 lb), peeled and sliced into 3 mm (⅛ inch) rounds
200 ml (7 fl oz) unsweetened almond milk
finely grated zest of 1 lemon
2 garlic cloves, finely chopped
1 teaspoon dried rosemary

½ teaspoon chilli flakes
sea salt flakes
freshly ground black pepper
250 g (9 oz) ready-cooked beetroot (beets)
2 tablespoons nutritional yeast
1 handful grated non-dairy cheese

Heat the oven to 180°C (350°F/Gas 4). Lightly oil a 20 cm (8 inch) square ovenproof dish.

In a mixing bowl, combine the sweet potatoes, milk, lemon zest, garlic, rosemary, chilli flakes and salt and pepper. Toss to coat and set aside for 20 minutes.

Arrange a closely packed single layer of the sweet potato slices in the bottom of the prepared ovenproof dish, shaking off and reserving any excess milk. Add a layer of beetroot slices, then scatter over some of the nutritional yeast. Repeat the layering, finishing with sweet potato. Drizzle over just enough of the milk left in the bottom of the mixing bowl – a scant few tablespoons – to moisten. Cover tightly with foil and bake for 50 minutes, or until the sweet potato is tender when a skewer is inserted into the centre.

Remove from the oven, sprinkle over enough grated cheese to cover the top, and put under a hot grill (broiler) until the cheese is bubbling and golden. Leave in dish for 5 minutes before serving.

roast spiced pumpkin

WITH BRAISED LENTILS & VINAIGRETTE

Meat eaters and non-meat eaters alike love this. Serve with
a selection of dishes as part of a buffet spread.

SERVES: 2 as a main or 4 as a side dish
PREPARATION: 30 minutes
COOKING: 45 minutes

**1 butternut pumpkin (squash),
about 750 g (1 lb 10 oz)**
150 ml (5 fl oz) olive oil
1 teaspoon ground cumin
1 teaspoon hot smoked paprika
sea salt flakes
freshly ground black pepper
1 garlic bulb, cloves separated, skin on
2 medium onions, finely sliced

½ fennel bulb, finely sliced
250 g (9 oz) puy lentils, rinsed
1 litre (35 fl oz/4 cups) strong vegetable stock
2 bay leaves
4 thyme sprigs
2 tablespoons hazelnut oil
3 tablespoons red wine vinegar
1 handful baby English spinach

Heat the oven to 180°C (350°F/Gas 4). Cut the
squash in half lengthways and remove the seeds.
Slice into 1.5 cm (⅝ inch) wedges and arrange in
a baking tray. Whisk together 3 tablespoons of the
olive oil, the cumin, paprika and salt and pepper.
Pour over the squash and turn to coat. Add the
garlic cloves and roast for about 45 minutes, or
until the squash is tender. Squeeze the garlic flesh
out of the skins, mash with a fork and set aside.

Meanwhile, heat 3 tablespoons of the olive oil in a
pan and add the onions and fennel. Stir to coat in
the oil, reduce the heat to medium–low and cook
for 8 minutes, or until tender. Stir in the lentils
and add the stock, bay leaves and thyme. Simmer
gently for about 25 minutes, or until *al dente*.
Drain, reserving any cooking liquor left in the pan,
and set aside.

While the lentils are cooking, make the dressing
by whisking together the remaining olive oil, the
hazelnut oil, vinegar and salt and pepper.

Stir the mashed garlic and most of the dressing
into the lentils. Gently warm through over a low
heat. Add a little of the reserved cooking liquid
so that the lentils are bathed in a lovely sauce.
Taste for seasoning. Stir through the spinach until
wilted, then remove from the heat.

To serve, tip the lentils onto a serving platter and
top with the pumpkin. Drizzle over the remaining
vinaigrette and serve immediately.

rich & creamy vegetable curry

Making curry paste might seem like a palaver but it's easy. Most of the work is done in the food processor and the flavour is deeper and fresher than shop-bought paste. This paste is quite mild so add another fresh red chilli and/or more chilli powder if you prefer more heat.

SERVES: 4–6
PREPARATION: 30 minutes
COOKING: 45 minutes

FOR THE CURRY PASTE
1 teaspoon cumin seeds
1 teaspoon coriander seeds
½ teaspoon mustard seeds
1 teaspoon hot chilli powder
1 tablespoon hot smoked paprika
2 garlic cloves
3 cm (1¼ inch) piece fresh root ginger, peeled and coarsely chopped
2 teaspoons garam masala
1 teaspoon sea salt flakes
2 tablespoons vegetable oil
2 tablespoons tomato paste (concentrated purée)
2 red chillies, finely chopped

FOR THE CURRY
200 g (7 oz) potatoes, chopped into 1 cm (½ inch) dice
2 medium sweet potatoes, about 400 g (14 oz), chopped into 1 cm (½ inch) dice
1 medium eggplant (aubergine), about 250 g (9 oz), chopped into 1 cm (½ inch) dice
75 ml vegetable oil
sea salt flakes
freshly ground black pepper
2 onions, finely chopped
350 ml (12 fl oz) tomato passata (puréed tomatoes)
400 ml (14 fl oz) coconut milk
1 medium zucchini (courgette), halved lengthways and cut into 5 mm (¼ inch) slices
chopped coriander (cilantro), to serve

To make the curry paste, toast the seeds in a dry frying pan until fragrant. The mustard seeds will start to pop when ready. Set aside to cool. Put the remaining paste ingredients in a mini food processor or mortar, add the cooled seeds and blitz or pound to a paste.

Heat the oven to 200°C (400°F/Gas 6). Toss the potatoes, sweet potatoes and eggplant with half the curry paste and 2 tablespoons of the vegetable oil in a large baking tray. Season with salt and pepper and roast for 30–40 minutes until the potato is tender.

Meanwhile, heat the remaining oil in a large pan and cook the onions, stirring frequently, over a medium–high heat until soft and starting to turn golden, about 8 minutes. Stir in the remaining curry paste and cook for 4 minutes more. Add the tomato passata and 150 ml (5 fl oz) water and cook, stirring, until the oil starts to separate from the sauce. Add the coconut milk and more salt and pepper. Add the roasted vegetables and the zucchini. Cook for 5 minutes. To serve, scatter with coriander and enjoy with basmati rice or vegan naan bread.

smoky mushroom stew

WITH BARLEY

This stew is dark, rich and almost meat-like, especially if you include shiitake in the mushroom mix. The mushrooms work exceptionally well with the barley, which has a slightly chewy texture and nutty taste.

SERVES: 2–4
PREPARATION: 15 minutes
COOKING: 30 minutes

650 ml (22½ fl oz) porcini mushroom stock (vegetable stock is fine)
200 g (7 oz/1 cup) pearled barley, rinsed
2 tablespoons olive oil
400 g (14 oz) mixed mushrooms, sliced
1 garlic clove, minced
1 tablespoon chopped thyme
1 tablespoon chopped flat-leaf (Italian) parsley, plus more for sprinkling

finely grated zest of ½ lemon, plus 1 squeeze lemon juice
sea salt flakes
freshly ground black pepper
3 tablespoons sweet Marsala
200 ml (7 fl oz) tomato passata (puréed tomatoes), plus extra if needed
1 teaspoon chipotle paste
1 pinch soft light brown sugar

In a large pan, bring the stock to the boil and add the barley. Cook for 20–25 minutes until tender, adding some water if the stock threatens to evaporate before the grains are cooked. By the end of cooking the stock should be completely absorbed and the grains tender but retaining some bite. Set aside to keep warm.

Meanwhile, heat the oil in a lidded pan and add the mushrooms, garlic, thyme, parsley and the lemon zest. Reduce the heat, cover and cook for 5 minutes. Turn up the heat, add the Marsala and

let it bubble away for a minute or so as you stir and scrape the bottom of the pan with a spoon. Cover, reduce the heat and cook for 10 minutes more. Add the passata, chipotle paste and sugar. Cook over a low heat with the lid off until you have a rich dark stew, about 5 minutes. Add a little more tomato passata if too thick. Stir in the squeeze of lemon juice and season well with salt and pepper.

Spoon the barley into serving bowls, top with the mushroom stew and serve sprinkled with parsley.

shepherd's pie

WITH PARSNIP & POTATO MASH

A rich mushroom and lentil stew topped with a cloud of flavoursome mash –
this dish is hard to beat when it comes to hearty, tasty fare.
Meat? Who needs it?

SERVES: 4–6
PREPARATION: 15 minutes
COOKING: 1 hour 20 minutes, plus 5 minutes cooling

1 kg (2 lb 4 oz) potatoes, peeled and quartered
400 g (14 oz) parsnips, peeled and cut into chunks
fine sea salt
150 ml (5 fl oz) non-dairy milk, warmed, plus a little more if needed for thinning
60 ml (2 fl oz/1/4 cup) olive oil
freshly ground black pepper
40 g (11/2 oz) dried porcini mushrooms
600 ml (21 fl oz) hot water
750 ml (26 fl oz/3 cups) porcini mushroom stock (vegetable stock is fine)

270 g (91/2 oz/11/4 cup) green or brown lentils, rinsed
2 bay leaves
1 onion, finely chopped
2 medium carrots, diced small
2 garlic cloves, minced
2 tablespoons chopped thyme
500 g (1 lb 2 oz) mushrooms, such as chestnut, portobello, oyster or wild, sliced
3 tablespoons tomato paste (concentrated purée)
100 g (31/2 oz/2/3 cup) frozen peas
1 tablespoon cornflour (cornstarch)

Cook the potatoes and parsnips in simmering salted water for 20 minutes, or until tender. Drain, return to the pan and mash with the warm milk and 2 tablespoons of the olive oil. Season with salt and pepper and set aside.

Cover the porcini mushrooms in the hot water and set aside. Meanwhile, simmer the stock, lentils and bay leaves for 20 minutes, or until tender. Drain off any excess water and discard the bay leaves.

Meanwhile, heat the remaining olive oil in a pan and fry the onion, carrot, garlic and thyme until soft and caramelised, about 15 minutes. Heat the oven to 180°C (350°F/Gas 4).

When the onion has almost finished cooking, drain the porcini mushrooms, reserve the soaking liquor and chop. Add to the onion mixture, then stir in the fresh mushrooms, tomato paste, peas and flour and cook for 1 minute. Add the porcini soaking liquor and lentils. The lentils and mushrooms should be bathed in sauce, so add a little water to loosen. Season generously with salt and pepper.

Pour lentil mixture into a 30 x 25 cm (12 x 10 inch) ovenproof dish. Spoon over the mash (beat in a little more milk if too thick) and spread it right up the edges with the back of a spoon. Bake for 40 minutes, or until bubbling and golden on top. Leave to stand in the ovenproof dish for 5 minutes before serving.

potato & spinach vindaloo

Your kitchen will smell wonderful while you make this spicy curry.
I am very happy to eat this without accompaniment
because it's so filling and satisfying.

SERVES: 2–4
PREPARATION: 20 minutes
COOKING: about 45 minutes

FOR THE CURRY PASTE
4 cardamom pods
2 teaspoons coriander seeds
1 teaspoon mustard seeds
1 teaspoon fennel seeds
2 cloves
3 teaspoons ground cumin
1 teaspoon ground cinnamon
2 teaspoons hot curry powder (use
1 teaspoon if you prefer a milder curry)
2 medium red chillies, seeded
and finely chopped
1 teaspoon fine sea salt
2 tablespoons tomato paste
(concentrated purée)
40 ml (1¼ fl oz) white wine vinegar
30 ml (1 fl oz) vegetable oil

FOR THE REST OF THE DISH
2 tablespoons vegetable oil
2 onions, chopped
175 g (6 oz) tin chopped tomatoes
1 tablespoon caster (superfine) sugar
1 teaspoon fine sea salt
650 g (1 lb 7 oz) boiling potatoes, peeled
and chopped into 3 cm (1¼ inch) dice
100 g (3½ oz) English spinach or
silverbeet (Swiss card)
chopped coriander (cilantro), to serve

For the curry paste, toast the cardamom pods
and the seeds in a dry frying pan until fragrant.
Transfer to a mortar, add the cloves and pound.
Discard the empty cardamom pods, shaking
out the seeds, and pound to a powder. Add the
remaining paste ingredients and pound to a wet
paste. Set aside.

Heat the vegetable oil in a large lidded pan
and gently cook the onions for 10 minutes, or
until very soft and golden at the edges. Add the
curry paste and stir for 3 minutes, being careful
not to burn the paste. Add 455 ml (16 fl oz) water,
the tomatoes, sugar and salt and gently simmer
for 10 minutes. Add the potatoes; they need to

be just covered with liquid, so top up with a little
water if necessary. Cover with the lid slightly
ajar and cook for 20 minutes. Remove the lid
and simmer for 10 minutes more, or until the
potatoes are tender and the sauce thick. Taste for
seasoning and add more salt or sugar if needed.

Add the spinach to the pan, cover and cook
until just wilted. If your pan is not large enough
to hold the curry and the spinach together, wilt
the spinach separately and then add. Gently stir
to combine the vegetables. Serve immediately,
sprinkled with coriander. Delicious with vegan
naan bread.

eggplant adobo stew

Eggplant soaks up the spicy, smoky flavour of adobo paste well. This recipe makes more paste than is needed for the stew because it's easier to do in this quantity, but it keeps for about three months, covered, in the fridge.

SERVES: 6
PREPARATION: 25 minutes, plus 30 minutes soaking
COOKING: 1 hour

2 medium eggplant (aubergines),
about 500 g (1 lb 2 oz), peeled and
chopped into bite-sized pieces
sea salt flakes
2 tablespoons rapeseed or vegetable oil
2 tablespoons olive oil
2 medium onions, chopped
2 x 400 g (14 oz) tins chopped tomatoes
1/2 teaspoon caster (superfine) sugar
1 squeeze lime juice, or more to taste
freshly ground black pepper
soya yoghurt or dairy-free cream
cheese, to serve
chopped coriander (cilantro), to serve

FOR THE ADOBO PASTE
4 chipotle or 2 ancho chillies
100 g (3 1/2 oz) tomato paste
(concentrated purée)
1 teaspoon agave nectar
1/2 onion, finely chopped
2 garlic cloves, finely chopped
1/2 teaspoon ground cinnamon
1 clove, ground
1/2 teaspoon dried oregano
1/2 teaspoon ground cumin
50 ml (2 1/2 tbsp) red wine vinegar

Heat the oven to 200°C (400°F/Gas 6). For the adobo paste, put the chipotle or ancho chillies in a bowl, cover with boiling water and set aside for 30 minutes. Make sure the chillies are submerged – you might need to weigh them down with a saucer.

Meanwhile, put the eggplant in a single layer in a large baking tray, sprinkle with salt, drizzle with the rapeseed or vegetable oil and toss to coat. Roast for 20 minutes, giving the tray a shake a couple of times during cooking.

Drain the chillies, remove and discard the stalks and put in a food processor. Add the remaining paste ingredients and blitz until smooth. Set aside.

Heat the olive oil in a large lidded pan, add the onions and cook for 10 minutes, or until soft and golden. Stir in 90 ml (3 fl oz) of the adobo paste and cook for a couple of minutes. Add the tomatoes and sugar and stir in 400 ml (14 fl oz) water. Add the eggplant, stirring to ensure all the pieces are submerged. Gently simmer with the lid on but slightly ajar for 25 minutes. Add the lime juice and season with salt and pepper.

Serve with a spoonful of yoghurt or cream cheese and a sprinkling of coriander. Delicious with steamed rice.

crispy crumbed tofu

WITH CURRY SAUCE

This is based on a hugely popular Japanese dish that uses crumbed chicken or pork fillets. I think the tofu works exceptionally well.

SERVES: 4–6
PREPARATION: 30 minutes
COOKING: 45 minutes

FOR THE CURRY SAUCE
3 tablespoons vegetable oil
1 onion, chopped
4 garlic cloves, finely chopped
1 small piece fresh ginger, peeled and finely grated
3 carrots, diced small
2 tablespoons plain (all-purpose) flour
1 tablespoon medium curry powder
1 teaspoon garam masala
1 pinch dried chilli flakes
600 ml (21 fl oz) hot vegetable stock
3 teaspoons soft light brown sugar
2 tablespoons soy sauce

FOR THE REST OF THE DISH
700 g (1 lb 9 oz) extra firm tofu, drained and pressed (see p 15)
50 ml (2½ tbsp) non-dairy milk
4 tablespoons plain (all-purpose) flour
120 g (4¼ oz/2 cups) panko breadcrumbs
sea salt flakes
freshly ground black pepper
1 teaspoon smoked paprika
vegetable oil, for frying

For the sauce, heat the vegetable oil in a lidded pan and cook the onion, garlic and ginger until soft. Add the carrots, reduce the heat and sweat for 10 minutes with the lid on. Add the flour, curry powder, garam masala and chilli and cook for 2 minutes. Stir in the stock, sugar and soy. Bring to the boil, reduce the heat and simmer for 20 minutes, or until thick. Purée in a blender or push through a sieve if you prefer a smooth sauce. Alternatively, leave the sauce chunky. Set aside.

Cut the pressed tofu into 1 cm (½ inch) slices. Put the milk, flour and breadcrumbs in separate shallow bowls. Season the flour with salt and pepper and mix the paprika into the breadcrumbs. Dip a slice of tofu in the flour, then in the milk and finally dredge in the breadcrumbs. Repeat for the rest of the tofu. Heat enough vegetable oil in a frying pan to come 5 cm (2 inches) up the sides and fry the crumbed tofu over a medium–high heat until golden on both sides. Remove and drain on paper towels.

Serve the tofu with the curry sauce spooned over or on the side for guests to help themselves.

eggplant parmigiana

This is a vegan spin on the gorgeous Italian classic, and one of my favourites.

SERVES: 4 as a main
PREPARATION: 15 minutes
COOKING: 50 minutes

3 tablespoons olive oil, plus extra for brushing
1 onion, finely chopped
1 garlic clove, sliced
800 ml (28 fl oz) tomato passata (puréed tomatoes)
1 teaspoon caster (superfine) sugar
2 teaspoons dried oregano
sea salt flakes

freshly ground black pepper
3 eggplant (aubergines), about 650 g (1 lb 7 oz)
3 tablespoons vegan parmesan cheese, home-made (*see* p 102) or grated shop-bought
50 g (1¾ oz) non-dairy cheese, grated
60 g (2¼ oz) breadcrumbs
basil leaves, to serve (optional)

Heat 2 tablespoons of the oil in a heavy pan and cook the onion over a medium heat for 10 minutes, or until soft and golden. Add the garlic and cook for 2 minutes more. Stir in the tomato passata, sugar, oregano and salt and pepper. Let the sauce bubble up, then reduce the heat to low. Cover and simmer gently for 15 minutes.

Meanwhile, cut the eggplant into 1 cm (½ inch) rounds and brush both sides with oil. Heat a griddle pan over a high heat and grill the eggplant on both sides until tender and charred.

Heat the oven to 190°C (375°F/Gas 5). Spoon one-third of the tomato sauce into an ovenproof dish about 25 x 20 cm (10 x 8 inches). Sprinkle over 1 tablespoon of the parmesan cheese, then add half the eggplant slices. Repeat the layering, finishing with tomato sauce and parmesan cheese. Sprinkle over the cheese, then the breadcrumbs. Drizzle with the remaining oil. Bake for 25 minutes, or until the top is golden and the sauce bubbling. Leave to stand in the dish for 5 minutes, then serve scattered with basil leaves (if using).

smoky three-bean chilli

The wonderful richness of this spicy chilli makes the absence of meat irrelevant. I've used three different types of beans here because the contrast looks and tastes wonderful. It's quite spicy.

SERVES: 4
PREPARATION: 15 minutes, plus 20 minutes soaking
COOKING: 40 minutes

2 tablespoons olive oil
1 onion, finely chopped
2 garlic cloves, finely chopped
1 medium red chilli, finely sliced
1 teaspoon chopped or
3 teaspoons dried oregano
1 teaspoon ground cumin
2 teaspoons smoked paprika
1 teaspoon chilli powder
2 chipotles, rehydrated in hot water for
20 minutes, seeded and chopped
1 x 400 g (14 oz) tinned black beans, drained
and rinsed

1 x 400 g (14 oz) tinned kidney beans, drained and rinsed
1 x 400 g (14 oz) tinned cannellini beans, drained and rinsed
1 x 400 g (14 oz) tin chopped tomatoes
2 tablespoons tomato paste (concentrated purée)
300 ml (10½ fl oz) porcini mushroom or vegetable stock, plus 150 ml (5 fl oz) more if needed
juice of ½ lime, plus lime wedges, to serve
sea salt flakes
freshly ground black pepper
dairy-free sour cream, to serve

In a large pan, heat the oil and fry the onion over a medium heat for 7 minutes. Add the garlic and chilli and cook for 3 minutes more. Add the oregano, cumin, paprika, chilli powder and chipotles. Stir and cook for a few minutes more.

Add the beans, tomatoes, tomato paste and stock. Gently simmer, uncovered, for 30 minutes, stirring every so often to prevent the beans from sticking to the bottom of the pan.

Stir in the lime juice and season with salt and pepper. Keep tasting to make sure the seasoning is right as beans need lots of salt.

Serve topped with a splodge of sour cream and lemon wedges. Fantastic with steamed rice.

tomato & eggplant filo bake

Many people believe filo pastry must be brushed with melted butter, but olive oil works just as well. This dish is a little bit like a savoury baklava.

SERVES: 4–6
PREPARATION: 10 minutes
COOKING: 35 minutes

FOR THE FILO
4 tablespoons olive oil, for brushing,
plus extra for oiling
16 filo pastry sheets

FOR THE EGGPLANT FILLING
400 g (14 oz) eggplant (aubergine), coarsely chopped
½ tablespoon fine sea salt
2 flax eggs (*see* p 17)
80 g (2¾ oz) breadcrumbs
50 g (1¾ oz) non-dairy cheese, grated
2 tablespoons chopped basil
100 ml (3½ fl oz) olive oil
2 garlic cloves, crushed
2 tablespoons chopped flat-leaf (Italian) parsley
25 g (1 oz) sultanas (golden raisins)

2 tablespoons pine nuts
sea salt flakes
freshly ground black pepper

FOR THE TOMATO FILLING
100 ml (3½ fl oz) olive oil, plus extra for oiling
2 onions, finely sliced
2 garlic cloves
2 tablespoons tomato paste (concentrated purée)
8 ripe tomatoes, about 1 kg (2 lb 4 oz),
skinned and chopped
1 pinch caster (superfine) sugar
2 tablespoons chopped oregano
100 g (3½ oz) shelled broad beans, fresh or frozen
sea salt flakes
freshly ground black pepper

Lightly oil an ovenproof dish measuring 30 x 20 cm (12 x 8 inches) or similar. Trim the filo sheets to fit into the base. Cover with a clean, damp tea towel (dish towel) and set aside.

Put the eggplant in a colander, sprinkle with the salt and set over a bowl for 20 minutes to drain. Rinse, then pat dry.

Meanwhile, make the tomato filling. Heat 2 tablespoons of the oil in a large pan and cook the onions over a medium heat until very soft and golden. Add the garlic and tomato paste and cook for a few minutes more. Add the tomatoes, sugar and oregano and simmer for 10 minutes. Add the beans, season with salt and pepper and cook for 5 minutes more. Set aside.

To make the eggplant filling, put the eggplant in a food processor and roughly mince. Transfer to a mixing bowl and add the flax eggs, breadcrumbs, cheese, basil, the olive oil, garlic, parsley, sultanas, pine nuts and salt and pepper. Stir.

Heat the oven to 200°C (400°F/ Gas 6). Brush 4 sheets of the filo with oil and layer one on top of the other. Put the oiled sheets in the baking tray and spread the tomato mixture on top. Make another 4-sheet layer of filo as before and put on top. Cover with the eggplant mixture. Make a final 4-sheet filo layer and put on top. Brush with oil and bake for 35 minutes, or until golden and cooked through. Serve hot.

vegetable crumble

Resoundingly satisfying and filling, this creamy one-pot dish is the perfect family meal. Don't be deterred by the number of onions: they are sweet, delicious and a tasty reminder of how neglected a vegetable they are.

SERVES: 4
PREPARATION: 20 minutes
COOKING: 40 minutes, once the cheese sauce is made

90 ml (3 fl oz) olive oil, plus extra for oiling
650 g (1 lb 7 oz) pearl onions, peeled but left whole
250 g (9 oz) kale, sliced, tough stalks removed
2 garlic cloves, finely chopped
1 quantity cheese sauce (see p 103)
a splash of vegan white wine (optional)
1 x 400 g (14 oz) tinned cannellini beans, drained and rinsed

1 tablespoon chopped thyme or 1 teaspoon dried thyme
finely grated zest of 1 lemon
sea salt flakes
freshly ground black pepper
150 g (5½ oz) ciabatta or sourdough, torn
1 tablespoon nutritional yeast

Heat 2 tablespoons of the olive oil in a pan and cook the onions over a medium heat, shaking the pan frequently, until browned. Add a splash of water and reduce the heat to very low. Cover and sweat for a further 10 minutes, or until soft.

Meanwhile, heat 2 tablespoons of the olive oil in a frying pan and add the kale and garlic. Stir-fry over a medium–high heat until the kale is tender, about 1 minute. Set aside.

Heat the oven to 190°C (375°F/Gas 5). Warm the cheese sauce, adding a splash of wine or a little water to achieve the consistency of double cream.

In a large mixing bowl, gently combine the cheese sauce, onions, kale, beans, thyme, lemon zest and salt and pepper. Taste for seasoning: beans need lots of salt. Transfer to a lightly oiled ovenproof dish measuring 25 x 18 cm (10 x 7 inches) or similar.

Blitz the ciabatta or sourdough in a blender or food processor to crumbs. Add the nutritional yeast and remaining olive oil and pulse to combine. Sprinkle the crumbs over the creamy vegetables to completely cover. Cook for 25–30 minutes until the top is golden and the sauce bubbling. Serve immediately.

pastry

+++ +++

Start these delicious galettes and the quiche by making the basic pastry recipe on p 36, and prepare the fillings while the dough rests in the fridge. Each recipe makes 2 galettes, except for the quiche, which makes 1.

 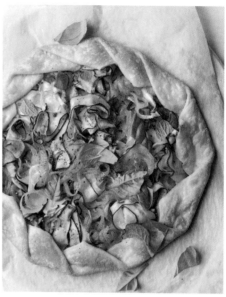 

WILD MUSHROOM GALETTES

Sauté 600 g (1 lb 5 oz) sliced mushrooms in olive oil until soft. Add 2 finely chopped garlic cloves and fry for 3 minutes. Add a splash of vegan white wine and stir. Add 3 tbsp chopped flat-leaf (Italian) parsley, a squeeze of lemon juice, a pinch of chilli flakes and season with salt and pepper. Roll the dough into 2 x 25 cm (10 inch) circles directly onto sheets of baking paper. Spoon the mushrooms on top, leaving a 3 cm (1¼ inch) border. Fold the border over, pleating and pressing to form a neat edge. Slide the galettes on their paper onto baking trays and bake for 25 minutes in a 180°C (350°F/Gas 4) oven.

ZUCCHINI & HERB GALETTES

Peel 4 zucchini (courgettes) and make ribbons with a vegetable peeler. Fry 2 sliced onions in olive oil until soft. Add the zucchini and 1 squeeze lemon juice and fry until tender. Add the grated zest of ½ lemon and some salt and pepper. Roll the dough into 2 x 25 cm (10 inch) circles directly onto sheets of baking paper. Spoon the zucchini mixture on top, leaving a 3 cm (1¼ inch) border. Fold the border over, pleating and pressing to form a neat edge. Slide the galettes on their paper onto baking trays and bake for 25 minutes in a 180°C (350°F/Gas 4) oven. Serve scattered with chopped mint and basil and a drizzle of extra virgin olive oil.

ASPARAGUS & GARLIC GALETTES

Very gently simmer the peeled cloves of 4 garlic bulbs in olive oil for 40 minutes. Remove and mash to a paste. Roll the dough into 2 x 25 cm (10 inch) circles directly onto baking paper. Spread the garlic paste over the dough, leaving a 3 cm (1¼ inch) border. Top with 200 g (7 oz) fine asparagus spears (slice thicker spears lengthways) and scatter with grated non-dairy cheese. Fold the border over, pleating and pressing to form a neat edge. Drizzle with olive oil and slide the galettes on their paper onto baking trays. Bake for 25 minutes in a 180°C (350°F/Gas 4) oven.

TOMATO & RICOTTA GALETTES

Make the ricotta recipe on p 102 and mix in 1 tsp dried oregano. Roll the dough out into 2 x 25 cm (10 inch) circles directly onto baking paper. Spread the ricotta over the dough, leaving a 3 cm (1¼ inch) border. Put halved cherry tomatoes cut-side up, covering the ricotta completely. Drizzle with olive oil and season with salt and pepper. Fold the border over, pleating and pressing to form a neat edge. Slide the galettes on their paper onto baking trays and bake for 25 minutes in a 180°C (350°F/Gas 4) oven.

SPINACH & CAPSICUM QUICHE

Use half the pastry recipe to line a 20 cm (8 inch) tart (flan) tin. Prick with a fork, chill for 30 minutes and bake for 10 minutes in a 180°C (350°F/Gas 4) oven. Fry 1 sliced onion in olive oil for 5 minutes. Add 2 chopped garlic cloves, 1 chopped yellow capsicum (pepper) and 1 tsp dried oregano. Fry until tender. Add 100 g (3½ oz) baby English spinach and fry until wilted. Set aside. In a blender, blitz 600 g (1 lb 5 oz) firm tofu and 2 tbsp nutritional yeast. Mix together the tofu, vegetables and 1 tbsp each chopped chives and basil. Pour into the pastry case and bake for 30–40 minutes until golden. Leave in the tin for 5 minutes before serving.

BEETROOT GALETTES

Add 2 tsp toasted caraway seeds to the basic pastry recipe. Fry 2 sliced onions in olive oil until soft. Add 1 tbsp balsamic vinegar and a pinch of sugar and fry for 3 minutes. Roll the dough into 2 x 25 cm (10 inch) circles directly onto baking paper. Spread the onion over the pastry circles, leaving a 3 cm (1¼ inch) border. Slice 200 g (7 oz) cooked beetroot (beets) and arrange on top of the onion. Fold the border over, pleating and pressing to form a neat edge. Slide the galettes on their paper onto baking trays and bake for 25 minutes in a 180°C (350°F/Gas 4) oven.

CHAPTER 8

sweet things

+ + +

vanilla cupcakes

+++ +++

MAKES: 10
PREPARATION: 15 minutes
COOKING: 15–18 minutes

FOR THE CUPCAKES
250 ml (9 fl oz/1 cup) non-dairy milk
1 teaspoon lemon juice
200 g (7 oz/1⅓ cups) self-raising flour
¾ teaspoon bicarbonate of soda (baking soda)
1 generous pinch fine sea salt
80 ml (2½ fl oz/⅓ cup) vegetable oil
150 g (5½ oz/⅔ cup) caster (superfine) sugar
1 teaspoon vanilla extract

FOR THE ICING (FROSTING)
100 g (3½ oz) non-dairy butter, softened
200 g (7 oz) icing (confectioners') sugar, sifted
¼ teaspoon vanilla extract
sugar sprinkles (optional)

Heat the oven to 180°C (350°F/Gas 4). Line 10 holes of a large muffin tray with paper cases.

Combine the milk and lemon juice and set aside. The milk might curdle – this is normal. Whisk together the flour, bicarbonate of soda and salt. In a separate bowl, beat the oil, sugar and vanilla together until well combined.

Add spoonfuls of the flour mixture to the oil and sugar mixture, alternating with the lemony milk, until just combined. Distribute the batter equally between the paper cases. Bake for 15–18 minutes until firm to the touch. Leave to cool in the tray for 5 minutes, then transfer to a wire rack to cool.

For the icing, beat together the ingredients until creamy. Chill until required. Spoon a dollop of the icing on top of each cake and spread out with the back of a spoon or a small blunt knife. Scatter with sprinkles if you are feeling fancy.

chocolate fudge torte

This scrumptious cake has a dense, damp and fudgy texture that makes it very moreish. It's quite rich so I suppose you could omit the icing. But if you're on a chocolate mission I'm not sure why you would.

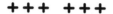

MAKES: 1 x 20 cm (8 inch) torte
PREPARATION: 10 minutes
COOKING: about 35 minutes, plus a couple of hours cooling

4 tablespoons vegetable oil,
plus extra for oiling
200 ml (7 fl oz) almond milk
1 tablespoon cider vinegar
250 g (9 oz/1²⁄₃ cups) plain (all-purpose) flour
50 g (1¾ oz) cocoa powder
1 teaspoon bicarbonate of soda (baking soda)
225 g (8 oz) caster (superfine) sugar
½ teaspoon fine sea salt
1 tablespoon hazelnut oil (vegetable oil is fine)

50 ml (2½ tbsp) cold espresso coffee
1½ teaspoons vanilla extract

FOR THE ICING (FROSTING)
150 ml (5 fl oz) almond milk
100 g (3½ oz) dairy-free chocolate,
broken into pieces
2 tablespoons agave nectar or maple syrup,
or more to taste

Heat the oven to 180°C (350°F/Gas 4). Oil a 20 cm (8 inch) cake tin and line the base with baking paper.

Mix together the milk and vinegar and set aside. In a mixing bowl, whisk together the flour, cocoa powder, bicarbonate of soda, sugar and salt. In a separate bowl, combine the vegetable oil and the hazelnut oil, coffee, vanilla and the milk mixture, which will have curdled and slightly thickened by now.

Gradually stir the wet ingredients into the dry, whisking to remove any lumps. Scrape into the prepared tin and bake for 25–30 minutes, or until the top feels firm.

Leave to stand in the tin for 5 minutes, then turn out onto a wire rack to cool.

To make the icing, heat the milk in a small pan until almost boiling. Remove from the heat and add the chocolate. Stir until all the chocolate is melted and the mixture smooth. Add the 2 tablespoons agave or maple syrup, or more to taste. Set aside for 10 minutes to thicken slightly.

When the cake is completely cool, sit it on its rack over a baking tray or board to catch any icing that runs off. Pour the icing over the cake, smoothing it around the side. Leave the icing to set before serving, or serve immediately.

carrot cake

WITH LEMONY ICING

Dark and rich with lots of juicy fruit, this is carrot cake heaven.
The crumb is deliciously moist so icing isn't strictly necessary,
but a swirl of lemony icing on top is a bonus.

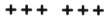

MAKES: 1 x 22 cm (8½ inch) cake
PREPARATION: 15 minutes
COOKING: about 45 minutes, plus a couple of hours cooling

300 ml (10½ fl oz) vegetable oil,
plus extra for oiling
300 g (10½ oz/2 cups) self-raising flour
3 teaspoons mixed spice
1 teaspoon baking powder
½ teaspoon bicarbonate of soda (baking soda)
275 g (9¾ oz) light muscovado or
soft light brown sugar
2 flax eggs (see p 17)
150 g (5½ oz) coarsely grated carrots
60 g (2¼ oz/¾ cup) sultanas (golden raisins)
100 g (3½ oz) tin chopped pineapple

FOR THE ICING (FROSTING)
60 g (2¼ oz) non-dairy butter, softened
200 g (7 oz) icing (confectioners') sugar, sifted
lemon juice, to taste
grated zest of ½ lemon
½ teaspoon vanilla extract
1 splash non-dairy milk, if needed

Heat the oven to 170°C (325°F/Gas 3). Oil a
22 cm (8½ inch) cake tin and line the base
with baking paper.

Whisk together the flour, mixed spice, baking
powder, bicarbonate of soda and sugar. In a
separate bowl, combine the flax eggs and oil.

Stir the wet mixture into the dry until well
combined. Fold in the carrots, sultanas and
pineapple. Scrape into the prepared tin and
bake for about 45 minutes, or until a skewer

inserted into the centre comes out clean.
Leave to rest in the tin for 5 minutes, then turn
out onto a wire rack to cool.

To make the icing, beat the butter until creamy.
Beat in the icing sugar, then the lemon juice,
lemon zest and vanilla. Add a splash of milk to
loosen if too thick. Once the cake is completely
cold, swirl the icing over the top and side.

orange & olive oil syrup cake

WITH CARDAMOM

Fragrant, dense and doused in syrup, this is wonderful either warm or cold.
If you don't want to add the orange slices on top, feel free to omit that step.

MAKES: 1 x 22 cm (8½ inch) cake
PREPARATION: 15 minutes
COOKING: 50 minutes, plus 1 hour for simmering the orange slices

100 ml (3½ fl oz) mild olive oil,
plus extra for oiling
3 oranges
425 g (15 oz) caster (superfine) sugar, plus
3 tablespoons extra for the syrup
about 100 ml (3½ fl oz) non-dairy milk

1 teaspoon vanilla extract
20 cardamom pods
225 g (8 oz/1½ cups) self-raising flour
1 teaspoon baking powder
½ teaspoon fine sea salt

Heat the oven to 170°C (325°F/Gas 3). Lightly oil a 22 cm (8½ inch) loose-bottomed cake tin and line the base with baking paper.

Finely slice 1 orange, skin on. Put 200 g (7 oz) of the sugar in a pan, add 200 ml (7 fl oz) water and stir to dissolve. Add the orange slices and simmer gently for about 1 hour, or until the skins are translucent. Remove from the syrup with a slotted spoon and arrange neatly in the base of the prepared tin.

Meanwhile, peel and chop 1 of the oranges and blitz the flesh to a pulp in a blender. Pour into a measuring jug, add all of the oil and enough of the milk to make 300 ml (10½ fl oz) of liquid. Add the vanilla.

Crush the cardamom pods in a mortar or bash with a rolling pin. Remove the seeds and crush to a powder. In a mixing bowl, combine the flour, baking powder, salt, remaining sugar and half the ground cardamom. Finely grate the zest of the remaining orange and add to the bowl, reserving the rest of the orange to juice later. Add the oil mixture and stir. Pour the batter over the orange slices in the prepared tin and bake for 45 minutes, or until a skewer inserted into the centre comes out clean.

While the cake is cooking, squeeze the reserved orange, pour the juice into a pan and add the 3 tablespoons sugar, 100 ml (3½ fl oz) water and the remaining ground cardamom. Simmer until reduced to a syrup.

When the cake is cooked, poke deep holes in the top with a chopstick. Pour over the syrup, getting as much into the holes as possible. Spoon any syrup that pools around the edges back over the cake. Let the cake stand for 5 minutes before inverting onto a plate. Remove from the tin and carefully peel off the paper to reveal the lovely orange slices. Enjoy warm or cold.

pistachio cake

WITH ORANGE BLOSSOM WATER

This is the perfect afternoon tea cake.

MAKES: 1 x 20 cm (8 inch) cake
PREPARATION: 20 minutes
COOKING: 55 minutes, plus a couple of hours cooling

160 ml (5¼ fl oz) vegetable oil, plus extra for oiling
250 g (9 oz) caster (superfine) sugar
180 ml soya yoghurt
1 teaspoon orange blossom water
1 teaspoon vanilla extract
2 tablespoons finely grated orange zest
100 g (3½ oz) shelled pistachio nuts, finely ground, plus extra, crushed, to decorate
200 g (7 oz/1⅓ cups) self-raising flour
30 g (1 oz/¼ cup) cornflour (cornstarch)

1 teaspoon baking powder
2 teaspoons ground cardamom
¼ teaspoon fine sea salt
120 ml soya milk

FOR THE ICING (FROSTING)
100 g (3½ oz) non-dairy butter, softened
200 g (7 oz) icing (confectioners') sugar, sifted
½ teaspoon orange blossom water
½ teaspoon vanilla extract
1 squeeze lemon

Heat the oven to 160°C (315°F/Gas 2–3). Oil a 20 cm (8 inch) cake tin and line the base with baking paper.

Beat the oil and sugar together until well combined. Add the yoghurt, orange blossom water, vanilla and orange zest and beat until incorporated. Set aside.

In a separate bowl, whisk together the ground pistachio nuts, the flours, baking powder, ground cardamom and salt. Gradually add the yoghurt mixture to the flour mixture, alternating with the milk and stirring between each addition until smooth. Be careful not to overbeat.

Pour into the prepared tin and bake for about 55 minutes, or until a skewer inserted into the centre comes out clean. If the top starts to brown too much before the cake is cooked, loosely cover with foil. Let the cake stand in the tin for 5 minutes, then turn out onto a wire rack to cool.

Meanwhile, beat together all the icing ingredients until smooth and creamy. Chill until needed but remove from the fridge 10 minutes before using. When the cake is completely cold, smooth the icing over the top and side and sprinkle with the crushed pistachio nuts.

peanut butter caramel swirl brownies

Hand-on-heart, these are among the most delicious brownies I've ever made, vegan or otherwise. And I've made quite a lot.

MAKES: 16
PREPARATION: 20 minutes
COOKING: 45 minutes

FOR THE PEANUT BUTTER CARAMEL
160 ml (5¼ fl oz) coconut cream (the thick layer at the top of an unshaken tin of Thai coconut milk)
70 g (2½ oz) caster (superfine) sugar
4 tablespoons peanut butter
4 tablespoons agave nectar
1 teaspoon vanilla extract
¾ teaspoon fine sea salt

FOR THE BROWNIES
250 g (9 oz/1⅔ cups) plain (all-purpose) flour
350 g (12 oz) golden caster (superfine) sugar
90 g (3¼ oz) cocoa powder
1 teaspoon baking powder
1 teaspoon fine sea salt
250 ml (9 fl oz/1 cup) almond milk
2 flax eggs (see p 17)
250 ml (9 fl oz/1 cup) vegetable oil
1 teaspoon vanilla extract

Heat the oven to 180°C (350°F/Gas 4). Line a 20 cm (8 inch) square baking tray with foil, letting it overhang the edges.

To make the caramel, heat the cream in a small pan. Meanwhile, in a heavy pan off the heat, mix the sugar with 60 ml (2 fl oz/¼ cup) water until dissolved, then cook over a medium–high heat until the mixture turns pale amber. Swirl the pan but don't stir. Reduce the heat, add the warm cream, then whisk in the peanut butter, agave, vanilla and salt. Transfer to a bowl to cool and set aside.

For the brownies, whisk together the flour, sugar, cocoa, baking powder and salt. In a separate bowl, combine the remaining brownie ingredients.

Gradually beat the wet ingredients into the dry until smooth. Pour half the batter into the prepared tin, then drizzle over half the caramel mixture. Pour over the remaining batter, smoothing it with the back of a spoon. Swirl over the remaining caramel.

Bake for 35 minutes, or until firm to touch. Leave to stand in the tray for 10 minutes, then use the foil to lift out onto a chopping board. Cut into 16 squares. Serve warm or cold. Delicious with vanilla ice cream.

amaretti-style biscuits

Nibbled with coffee, served as petit fours or even blitzed to make a cheesecake base, these are versatile biscuits. If you prefer, omit the almond extract and add 1½ teaspoons ground ginger to the flour instead.

MAKES: 30
PREPARATION: 10 minutes
COOKING: 8–10 minutes

140 g (5 oz) plain (all-purpose) flour
½ teaspoon baking powder
1 pinch sea salt
½ teaspoon ground cinnamon
85 g (3 oz) dark muscovado or
soft dark brown sugar

a few turns of freshly ground black pepper
60 ml (2 fl oz/¼ cup) vegetable oil
2 tablespoons golden syrup (light treacle)
½ teaspoon vanilla extract
1 teaspoon almond extract

Heat the oven to 180°C (350°F/Gas 4). Line a baking tray with baking paper.

In a small bowl, whisk together the flour, baking powder, salt, cinnamon, sugar and pepper. In a separate bowl, whisk together the oil, golden syrup, vanilla and almond extract.

Pour the wet ingredients into the dry and stir to combine. Knead to amalgamate if you need to. Roll level teaspoonfuls of the dough into balls, put on the prepared baking tray and flatten into discs about 8 mm thick (³⁄₈ inch). Leave 3 cm (1¼ inches) between each disc as they spread out a bit during cooking.

Bake for 8–10 minutes, or until pale brown underneath. They will still be quite soft but will firm up as they cool, so don't be tempted to leave them in the oven too long. Leave on the baking tray for 5 minutes, then transfer to a wire rack to cool and harden.

minty lemon posset

WITH SHORTBREAD

This tangy pudding pairs beautifully with the buttery shortbread.
The quantities for the shortbread make more than you need, but leftovers
will keep in an airtight container for a couple of days. If they last that long.

MAKES: 4 possets and 15 shortbread
PREPARATION: 30 minutes, plus 2 hours 30 minutes chilling
COOKING: about 20 minutes, plus 10 minutes cooling

FOR THE POSSET
100 ml (3½ fl oz) lemon juice, plus finely
grated zest of 1 lemon
20 mint leaves
120 g (4¼ oz) caster (superfine) sugar
400 ml (14 fl oz) coconut cream (the thick
layer at the top of an unshaken tin of
Thai coconut milk)
2 teaspoons xanthan gum
raspberries, to serve

FOR THE SHORTBREAD
160 g plain (all-purpose) flour,
plus extra for dusting
80 g (2¾ oz) cornflour (cornstarch)
1 pinch salt
160 g non-dairy butter, softened
65 g caster (superfine) sugar,
plus extra for sprinkling
finely grated zest of ½ lemon

First, make the posset. Combine the lemon juice, zest, mint and sugar in a pan and gently simmer until the sugar has dissolved and the mixture has thickened into a syrup. In a separate pan, heat the coconut cream until warm and smooth. Strain the syrup into the cream, discarding the mint, and whisk to combine. Sprinkle over the xanthan gum and simmer for a couple of minutes, stirring constantly. Pour through a sieve to remove any lumps and divide between 4 ramekins. Chill for at least 2 hours to set.

Meanwhile, make the shortbread. Sift the flours and salt together. Beat the butter with the sugar and lemon zest until pale and creamy. Gradually add the flour, stirring between each addition. Bring the dough together with your hands and turn out onto a lightly floured work surface.

Lightly knead – don't overwork or the shortbread will be tough. Shape into a disc, wrap in baking paper and chill for 30 minutes.

Heat the oven to 170°C (325°F/Gas 3). On a lightly floured work surface, evenly roll out the dough to a thickness of 5 mm (¼ inch) and stamp out shapes with a cookie cutter – I used a 8 x 4 cm (3¼ x 1½ inch) rectangle. Put on a baking tray lined with baking paper and bake for about 18 minutes. The shortbread will barely take on any colour but will be firm to the touch. Sprinkle with sugar and leave to cool on the tray for 10 minutes before transferring to a wire rack to cool completely.

Serve the posset with raspberries and a piece of shortbread on the side.

fruit en papillote

WITH COCONUT CREAM

You can vary the fruit here but try to include berries as the juices make a delicious sauce. You can also ring the changes by swapping maple syrup for agave nectar, or add a tiny dash of orange blossom water to the cream.

SERVES: 4
PREPARATION: 20 minutes
COOKING: 25 minutes

1 x 400 ml (14 fl oz) tin coconut milk
1 large peach, stoned and quartered
2 apricots, stoned and halved
1 large nectarine, stoned and quartered
1 handful blueberries
2 tablespoons soft light brown sugar
2 tablespoons sweet Marsala or sweet wine
1 vanilla pod, split in half lengthways

2 cinnamon sticks, halved
2 star anise, halved
2 teaspoons unrefined coconut oil (solid is fine)
½ teaspoon vanilla extract
2 tablespoons agave nectar, or more to taste
4 tablespoons flaked almonds or coconut flakes, lightly toasted, to serve

Heat the oven to 200°C (400°F/Gas 6). Put the tin of coconut milk in the freezer.

Tear off 4 large rectangles of baking paper and spread out on a work surface. Put all the fruit in a bowl and toss with the sugar and Marsala. Scrape the seeds from the vanilla pod and stir into the fruit. Cut the vanilla pod in half crossways to make 4 pieces.

Divide the fruit and the sugary syrup in the bottom of the bowl between the pieces of paper. Put a piece of cinnamon stick, star anise, vanilla pod and ½ teaspoon of coconut oil on top of each pile of fruit. Bring the top and bottom edges of the paper together and tightly fold. Twist the ends together to make tight packets, leaving some air inside. Put the packets on a baking tray and roast for 25 minutes, or until the fruit is tender and oozing juices. Cooking time will vary according to the ripeness of the fruit, so pop the packets back in the oven if the fruit is not quite done.

Make the coconut cream by following the recipe on p 27, beating in the vanilla extract and agave to sweeten. Chill until ready to serve.

To serve, put the packets on individual plates and allow guests to open them up themselves. The smell of the spices as the packets open is wonderful. Let guests help themselves to the coconut cream and almonds or coconut flakes to sprinkle on top.

iced berries

WITH HOT WHITE CHOCOLATE SAUCE

This is a really simple but tasty pudding.
If you don't like coconut, just leave it out.

SERVES: 4
PREPARATION: 5 minutes
COOKING: 5 minutes

500 g (1 lb 2 oz) frozen raspberries,
blackberries or blueberries, or a mixture
200 ml (7 fl oz) soya milk
200 g (7 oz) dairy-free white chocolate,
broken into pieces
1 teaspoon vanilla extract

1–2 tablespoons desiccated (shredded)
coconut, plus extra to serve
2 tablespoons agave nectar,
plus extra to taste
sea salt flakes

Take the berries out of the freezer and distribute among 4 serving bowls. Do this now so the berries can defrost slightly while you make the sauce.

Heat the milk until almost boiling, remove from the heat and add the chocolate. Stir until melted, then add the vanilla, coconut, agave and 1 pinch salt. Taste and add more agave or salt if needed.

Pour the warm sauce over the frozen berries, sprinkle with coconut and serve immediately.

crème brûlée

This is very tasty but can easily be fancied-up by adding flavourings.
Pop blueberries into the ramekins before adding the custard, or stir
4 teaspoons of cocoa powder into the custard at the end of cooking.

SERVES: 4
PREPARATION: 20 minutes
COOKING: 10 minutes, plus 1 hour 15 minutes cooling and chilling

3 tablespoons cornflour (cornstarch)
1 x 400 ml (14 fl oz) tin coconut milk, shaken
2 tablespoons cashew cream (*see* p 26)
80 g (2¾ oz) caster (superfine) sugar, plus
4 teaspoons extra for sprinkling

¼ teaspoon ground cinnamon
1 vanilla pod, seeds scraped out,
pod reserved
5 cm (2 inch) strip lemon zest

Put the cornflour into a small bowl. Pour the coconut milk into a pan. Whisk over a medium heat until the milk and cream are completely amalgamated. Add the cashew cream, sugar, cinnamon, vanilla seeds and vanilla pod. Stir well to combine.

Stir a few tablespoons of the hot milk mixture into the cornflour to make a paste. Pour the paste into the milk mixture, add the lemon zest and stir continuously over a medium–low heat until thick and creamy, about 5 minutes. Remove the lemon zest and vanilla pod.

Pour into 4 ramekins, leave to cool for 15 minutes and then chill for at least 1 hour, or until set.

Sprinkle the top of each ramekin with 1 teaspoon sugar. Blast the sugar with a cook's blowtorch until bubbling and golden. Alternatively, put under a very hot grill (broiler). Return to the fridge to chill until ready to serve. Lovely served with berries or plain biscuits for dunking.

sticky mango & lime rice pudding

WITH TOASTED COCONUT

This is a non-dairy version of the delicious Thai classic. It's important to use glutinous or sticky rice to achieve the right consistency.

SERVES: 4
PREPARATION: 15 minutes
COOKING: 30 minutes

200 g (7 oz/1 cup) glutinous rice or pudding rice
1 x 400 ml (14 fl oz) tin coconut milk, shaken well
finely grated zest and juice of 1 lime
2 ripe mangoes, peeled, stoned and sliced

2 tablespoons agave nectar or rice syrup
1 tablespoon unrefined coconut oil
50 g (1¾ oz) desiccated (shredded) coconut
2 tablespoons caster (superfine) sugar
100 g (3½ oz/½ cup) soft light brown sugar

In a medium pan, combine the rice, coconut milk, lime zest and 500 ml (17 fl oz/2 cups) water. Bring to the boil, reduce the heat to medium and cook until the rice is tender, about 20 minutes.

While the rice is cooking, put half the mango, the agave or rice syrup, half the lime juice and 1 tablespoon water in a blender and blitz until smooth. Set aside.

Pour the remaining lime juice over the remaining mango slices and set aside.

In a frying pan, heat the coconut oil, add the coconut and caster sugar and cook, stirring constantly, until lightly browned and fragrant.

When the rice is cooked, remove from the heat and stir through the soft light brown sugar. Spoon into serving bowls and pour over some of the mango purée. Top the rice with mango slices and sprinkle with the toasted coconut. Serve immediately.

sautéed pears

WITH SALTED CARAMEL & PECANS

This stylish dessert is very easy, despite the stirring involved to reduce the coconut milk. Watch the pan like a hawk when you caramelise the sugar, and remember it will keep cooking after you take it off the heat.

+++ +++

SERVES: 4–6
PREPARATION: 10 minutes
COOKING: 30 minutes

1 x 400 ml (14 fl oz) tin coconut milk
100 g (3½ oz) caster (superfine) sugar
1 teaspoon vanilla extract
½ teaspoon sea salt flakes, or to taste

4 pears
2 tablespoons refined coconut oil
60 g (2¼ oz) pecans

Pour the coconut milk into a small pan and whisk to combine the cream and the milk. Briskly simmer over a medium heat, stirring constantly, until reduced by half, about 15 minutes. Set aside.

Put the sugar in a heavy pan, add 2 tablespoons cold water and mix well until combined. Set over a medium–high heat and cook without stirring until the mixture turns pale amber. Remove from the heat and carefully (the caramel will splatter!) stir in the reduced coconut milk, vanilla and salt. Return to a medium heat and let the caramel bubble away, stirring often, for about 5 minutes until thickened. Set aside.

Peel, quarter and core the pears. Heat the coconut oil in a large frying pan over a medium–high heat and add the pear pieces. Fry until golden on all sides, about 5 minutes. Add the pecans, shake the pan to coat in the juices and cook for a further 2 minutes.

To serve, arrange the pears on serving plates, spoon over the caramel sauce and scatter with the pecans. Serve immediately, while the pears and sauce are still warm.

strawberry cheesecake

+++ +++

SERVES: 8
PREPARATION: 10 minutes, plus 2 hours chilling
COOKING: 2 minutes

FOR THE BASE
80 g (2¾ oz) rolled (porridge) oats
80 g (2¾ oz/¾ cup) almond meal
2 tablespoons coconut oil, melted
3 tablespoons agave nectar
1 pinch salt

FOR THE FILLING
450 g (1 lb) silken tofu, drained
200 ml (7 fl oz) coconut cream (the thick layer at the top of an unshaken tin of Thai coconut milk)
1 teaspoon vanilla extract
1 teaspoon xanthan gum
4 tablespoons caster (superfine) sugar
1 tablespoon icing (confectioners') sugar, shifted, for dusting
300 g (10½ oz/2 cups) strawberries, hulled and halved

Put the oats in a food processor and blitz to a flour-like consistency. Add the remaining base ingredients and blitz again until combined. Tip into a 20 cm (8 inch) round or 35 x 11 cm (14 x 4¼ inch) springform cake tin and press evenly into the base using the back of a spoon. Chill.

Meanwhile, beat together all the filling ingredients except the icing sugar and strawberries, until thick and creamy. Spread over the cheesecake base, smoothing the top with a spatula. Chill for at least 2 hours in the tin.

Just before serving, carefully distribute the strawberries on top of the cheesecake and dust with the icing sugar. Release the cheesecake from the tin and serve.

cherry clafoutis

Fresh cherries work brilliantly in this French classic but berries also work well. In some regions of France, the cherry stones are left in to impart their distinctive flavour, but I prefer to remove them.

SERVES: 4–6
PREPARATION: 15 minutes
COOKING: about 1 hour

20 g (¾ oz) non-dairy butter, plus extra for greasing
90 g (3¼ oz) caster (superfine) sugar
400 g (14 oz/1⅔ cup) cherries, pitted
80 g (2¾ oz) self-raising flour
1 tablespoon cornflour (cornstarch)
2 tablespoons almond meal

1 pinch salt
2 flax eggs (see p 17)
270 ml (9½ fl oz) unsweetened almond milk
finely grated zest of 1 lemon
1 teaspoon vanilla extract
¼ teaspoon almond extract
icing (confectioners') sugar, sifted, for dusting

Heat the oven to 180°C (350°F/Gas 4). Grease a 25 cm (10 inch) round ovenproof dish with butter and sprinkle the base and side with 1 tablespoon of the sugar. Arrange the cherries in the dish in a single layer. Set aside.

Beat together the butter, remaining sugar, the flours, almond meal, salt, flax eggs, milk, lemon zest, vanilla and almond extract until smooth.

Pour the batter over the cherries and bake for about 1 hour – the clafoutis should be golden on top and just set. Serve warm, dusted with icing sugar.

ice cream

+++ +++

All these ideas for ice cream use a coconut milk base to provide creaminess and almond milk to smooth out the coconut flavour. The creamiest results are achieved in an ice-cream maker, but it's possible to make good ice cream by freezing the mixture for several hours, blitzing in a food processor, freezing for a further hour and then blitzing again just before serving. All the variations below serve 4.

CHOCOLATE (right)

Make the vanilla ice cream but add 4 tbsp unsweetened cocoa powder and 2 extra tbsp sugar when first combining the ingredients. Continue the recipe as for the vanilla ice cream.

VANILLA (left)

Beat 250 ml (9 fl oz/1 cup) coconut cream (the thick layer at the top of an unshaken tin of Thai coconut milk) with 250 ml (9 fl oz/1 cup) unsweetened almond milk, the seeds from 1 vanilla pod, 3 tbsp caster (superfine) sugar and 1 pinch salt. Whisk to dissolve the sugar. Put in an ice-cream maker and churn following to the machine directions. Alternatively, put in a freezer-proof container and freeze for 3–4 hours, then blitz in a food processor and freeze for 1 more hour. Blitz again just before serving.

SALTED CARAMEL (left)

Make the vanilla ice cream. While it's churning or freezing for the first time make the salted caramel. In a small pan, heat 90 g (3¼ oz) soft light brown sugar, 50 g (1¾ oz) non-dairy butter, 2 tbsp non-dairy milk and 2 tbsp coconut milk over a medium heat until dissolved. Increase the heat and gently boil for about 5 minutes. Remove from the heat, stir in ¼ tsp sea salt flakes and set aside to cool. After the ice cream has churned or been blitzed in the food processor, swirl through half of the caramel. Refreeze and continue the recipe as for the vanilla ice cream. Pour the remaining caramel over the ice cream to serve.

COCONUT (above)

Toast 2 tbsp desiccated (shredded) coconut in a dry frying pan until golden. Make the vanilla ice cream but don't use a mixture of coconut cream and almond milk. Instead, use the cream and milk from 1 x 400 g (14 oz) tin of Thai coconut milk. Add the toasted coconut when combining the ingredients and continue the recipe as for the vanilla ice cream.

BANANA (above)

Mash 4 ripe bananas. Make the basic vanilla ice cream and beat in the mashed bananas when combining the ingredients. Continue the recipe as for the vanilla ice cream.

RUM & RAISIN (right)

Soak 4 tbsp raisins in 3 tbsp sweet sherry or dark rum. Make the vanilla ice cream and stir through the raisins and soaking liquor after churning or blitzing for the first time. Continue the recipe as for the vanilla ice cream.

menu planner

+ + +

buffet party

Mediterranean terrine (p 68)

filled sweet potato skins (p 84)

lentil & cranberry salad (p 120)

orange-scented quinoa salad (p 122)

warm root veg & grain salad (p 134)

saffron roasted tomatoes with herbed tofu (p 144)

roasted tofu with African spices (p 150)

orange & olive oil syrup cake (p 224)

strawberry cheesecake (p 244)

drinks party

crudités with whipped garlic dip (p 74)

witlof cups with walnut tabouleh (p 72)

crispy polenta bites with green tapenade (p 76)

caraway seed pastries (p 78)

zucchini & farro fritters (p 86)

peanut butter caramel swirl brownies (p 228)

amaretti-style biscuits (p 230)

children's party

tutti fruiti smoothies (p 41)

toasted seaweed snacks (p 90)

cheese & spinach muffins (p 60)

vegetable fritters with dipping sauce (p 82)

pizzettes with mozzarella & onion relish (p 70)

vanilla cupcakes (p 218)

chocolate ice cream (p 248)

celebration dinner

crudités with whipped garlic dip (p 74)

Mediterranean terrine (p 68)

gnocchi with truffled cauliflower sauce (p 178)

dressed green leaves

sautéed pears with salted caramel & pecans (p 242)

vanilla ice cream (p 248)

relaxed brunch for a crowd

chocolate smoothies (p 40)

berry good smoothies (p 41)

breakfast burritos with refried beans (p 52)

scrambled tofu with black beans & spinach (p 54)

fruit loaf with apple butter (p 50)

fresh fruit platter

summer picnic

witlof cups with walnut tabouleh (p 72)

caraway seed pastries (p 78)

chilled watermelon & coriander salad (p 118)

Thai salad (p 124)

carrot cake with lemony icing (p 222)

weeknight family dinner

chorizo burgers (p 97)

matchstick salad (p 112)

banana ice cream with fresh fruit (p 249)

weekend lunch

corn chowder (p 104)

eggplant parmigiana (p 206)

warm root veg & grain salad (p 134)

cherry clafoutis (p 246)

amaretti-style biscuits (p 230)

index

+ + +

+ + +

acknowledgments

Thanks so much to Catie Ziller for giving me the chance to explore the wonderful world of vegan cooking. I have learned so much in the process.

I am also hugely grateful to food stylist Vivian Lui and photographer Victoria Wall Harris: they have turned a bunch of recipes into a truly gorgeous book. I am also indebted to Vivian for her helpful suggestions and attention to detail during the course of making these recipes for the shoot.

To Alice Chadwick, it's always lovely to work with you. I am constantly amazed at what a clever and original designer you are. I think the results here are stunning.

Finally, as ever, huge thanks to my happy band of recipe testers: Adam, Ruby and Ben. You did not choose to eat a mainly vegan diet for all those weeks, but did so happily, offering hugely helpful suggestions and support all the while.

To Adam, my supportive fetcher, carrier and sage: once again, it wouldn't have happened without you.

+ + +

Published in 2015 by Murdoch Books, an imprint of Allen & Unwin
Reprinted 2015, 2016, 2017 (thrice), 2018 (twice), 2019 (x2)
First published by Marabout in 2014

Murdoch Books Australia
83 Alexander Street,
Crows Nest NSW 2065
Phone: +61 (0)2 8425 0100
murdochbooks.com.au
info@murdochbooks.com.au

Murdoch Books UK
Ormond House,
26–27 Boswell Street,
London, WC1N 3JZ
Phone: +44 (0) 20 8785 5995
murdochbooks.co.uk
info@murdochbooks.co.uk

For Corporate Orders & Custom Publishing contact our business development team at salesenquiries@murdochbooks.com.au

Publisher: Corinne Roberts
Photographer: Victoria Wall Harris
Food Stylist: Vivian Lui
Props Stylist: Scott Horne
Illustrator & Designer: Alice Chadwick
Translator: Melissa McMahon
Editor: Jennifer Taylor
Production Director: Lou Playfair

Text and design copyright © Hachette Livre (Marabout) 2014
The moral rights of the author have been asserted.

A cataloguing-in-publication entry is available from the catalogue of the National Library of Australia at nla.gov.au

ISBN 978 1 74336 524 3 Australia
ISBN 978 1 74336 525 0 UK

A catalogue record for this book is available from the British Library

Colour reproduction by Splitting Image Colour Studio Pty Ltd, Clayton, Victoria
Printed by 1010 Printing International Limited, China

OVEN GUIDE: You may find cooking times vary depending on the oven you are using. For fan-forced ovens, as a general rule, set the oven temperature to 20°C (70°F) lower than indicated in the recipe.

MEASURES GUIDE: We have used 15 ml (3 teaspoon) tablespoon measures for recipes in this book.